Homestead Homilies

Homestead Homilies

Barry Blackstone

RESOURCE *Publications* • Eugene, Oregon

HOMESTEAD HOMILIES

Copyright © 2017 Barry Blackstone. All rights reserved. Except for brief quotations in critical publications or reviews, no part of this book may be reproduced in any manner without prior written permission from the publisher. Write: Permissions, Wipf and Stock Publishers, 199 W. 8th Ave., Suite 3, Eugene, OR 97401.

Resource Publications
An Imprint of Wipf and Stock Publishers
199 W. 8th Ave., Suite 3
Eugene, OR 97401

www.wipfandstock.com

PAPERBACK ISBN: 978-1-5326-1480-4
HARDCOVER ISBN: 978-1-5326-1482-8
EBOOK ISBN: 978-1-5326-1481-1

Manufactured in the U.S.A.   JANUARY 3, 2017

I dedicate these homestead homilies to the farm
companions of my youth;
with a heart-felt thanks for all the helpful instruction they
gave me that has sustained my faith through the years.

Others books by the author through Resource:

Though None Go with Me

Rendezvous in Paris

Though One Go with Me

Scotland Journey

The Region Beyond

Enlarge My Coast

From Dan to Beersheba and Beyond

The Uttermost Part

Contents

Introduction: Homestead Homilies | ix

1	Plowing Straight	1
2	Creation's Groan	3
3	Dawn's Dawning	5
4	Sad Succourer	7
5	Grandmother's Help	9
6	Morning Song	11
7	Sacred Sanctury	13
8	Weathering Weather	15
9	Plodding Plodder	17
10	Country Calm	19
11	Peaceful Place	21
12	Blessed Hope	23
13	Farmer's Psalm	25
14	Vivacious View	27
15	Perham Prayers	29
16	Family Preacher	31
17	Hallowed Hills	33
18	Blackstone Beekeeper	35
19	Chickadee Chorus	37
20	Farm Faith	39
21	Busybody Bees	41
22	Four Skies	43
23	Individual Influence	45
24	Worthy Walk	47

Contents

25	Fanner Bees	49
26	Young Giver	51
27	Farming Farmer	53
28	Admirable Afterglow	55
29	Good Gardener	57
30	Wonderful Wonder	59
31	Archer's Arrows	61
32	Land Lamentation	63
33	Dale Dew	65
34	Town Tragedy	67
35	Homestead Hedge	69
36	Sparrow Sounds	71
37	Lesser Light	73
38	Morning Moonset	75
39	Homestead Health	77
40	Four Seasons	79
41	Noontime Nap	81
42	Refreshing Rain	83
43	Summer Storm	85
44	Salutatorian Sylvia	87
45	Pump Priming	89
46	"Great" Grandmother	91
47	Devote Dad	93
48	Frosty Frost	95
49	Clover Concepts	97
50	Hill Homily	99

Conclusion: Soil Sermons | *101*

Introduction
Homestead Homilies

HAVING BEEN IN THE pastorate for over forty-three years now, I know what it means to be a pilgrim just passing through. Night has come and I am in my 4th church study. It is quiet and it is times like this I think of HOME; not Allenstown, New Hampshire, not Westfield, Maine, not Eastport, Maine, and not even Ellsworth, Maine where I live now, but Perham, Maine. No matter how far I roam (I have also travelled to India, Australia, Canada, Israel, France, England, and half of the United States), the Blackstone homestead will always be my earthly HOME; that is, until I exchange it for my heavenly HOME.

As I type the word HOME into my laptop, my mental computer begins to flash back to a HOME that has all but disappeared, except in my memory. The word floats through my mind as a pleasant place where the crickets still chirp and the frogs still croak in a cool evening breeze. My parent's house on the Russell Place still has an open porch, under which I created my own little world. My trucks and tractors still farm that small field hidden away behind mother's flower bed. The garage is still a wood shed, and Rover, my boyhood dog, is still chasing cats and cars in the front yard by the old cow barn; which burnt many years ago but still stands tall and strong against a stiff night's wind in my brain. Sparrows and swallows by the hundreds still make their nests in the grand structure, at least from where I'm reminiscing. In my mind's eyes I can see my wonderful sister Sylvia coming towards me and I hear her say,

Introduction

"Mum says it is too dark; it's time to come in!" I didn't want to leave then nor now, and in my thoughts I don't!

We live in an age where one's roots are said to be important, yet most don't even know who their parents are let alone their heritage. But I know of deep family roots! I know what a HOME really is. I was raised on a homestead farm, a real, genuine homestead. My great-great-great grandfather Hartson Blackstone carved my HOME out of a virgin forest, long before it was even called Perham, in 1861. My younger brother Jay was the sixth generation to turn the soil of that land. Roots like that run deep, deep into your very soul. No force this side of Heaven itself can pluck HOME from your brain or your body. Though I have now lived twice as long away, the urge and the ties to that place I call HOME is still overwhelming, so it is not surprising that on nights like this I feel I will dissolve into dust if I don't get back HOME.

A simple restart of my mind and memory and I am heading HOME. Perhaps, it is after a date with my wife-to-be Coleen (43 years passed), or a visit with Cousin Bob, a man already in his heavenly HOME (5 years passed). Or better still I am five again, and we are returning HOME from Sunday evening church (why I still have one in my church today). Sylvia and I are in the back of Dad's 56 Chevy, and the lights of my grandparent's car ahead of us have just turned onto the Blackstone Road as they head HOME. We continue on Route 228 out of Perham village as we make our way passed the old milking shed where the homestead herd of Holsteins was milked in the summertime. We enter the Sugar Woods as complete darkness overtakes Perham. Then as a lighthouse to a wandering mariner, we see the light from the old chicken coop in the back of the barn as we emerge from the forest. I can still hear my Dad say, "Well, the chickens are having a barn dance tonight!" My sister and I look at each other and smile. We know we are safe because we have made it safely HOME.

Little did I know then that my seminary training had already begun? It was not by chance or circumstance that I was raised on a farm with a pastor/farmer and a deacon/farmer. My grandfather Carroll and his brother Uncle Read farmed together for nearly forty

Introduction

years, and when they retired my father Wendell and his cousin Clayton took over. For 22 years I was under the influence of a close net Christian family with each member of that family contributing something to my seminary training. I learned about being a long-term pastor from Uncle Read (40 years in the same pastorate-I have pastored 25th at my certain church). I learned about being a man of integrity from my grandfather Carroll, the finest example of a Christian gentleman I have ever known. My father made it easy for me to trust and believe in the Heavenly Father by his sterling character as an earthly father. My two grandmothers taught me that you can keep the faith over the long term (Maude lived into her 90s and Glenna into her 100th year and both got saved early in life and never stopped believing-I often say I would be without excuse before the Almighty to depart or fall away from the faith simply because of my grandmother's testimony). And then there was mother, a prayer warrior extra-ordinary to say the least and the one that set me on the right course when I thought I knew God's way. Most seminaries last four years and by reason of higher education eight years or more, but I was in seminary for 22 years; a slow learner I guess! When I began to write in 1988, I realized and remembered many a "homestead homily" preached to me in my youth. I realized that my teachers were human and Holstein. My pastors were parents and pastures. My ministers were crops and cousins. My instructors were dogs and dandelions!

The homestead of my childhood has changed so dramatically that some feel I am imagining the things I write about. The Holstein herd is gone and so too the potato crop. Read and Carroll, Maude and Glenna have all moved to their homestead HOME in the sky. When I return and I often do (seven years ago I was given my grandparent's HOME on the homestead-it sets on seven acres of prime farmland-a constant reminder of my past), I hear little of what I once heard, and I see little of what I once saw. There is little that remains of my 'childhood college' except for a few elderly folks ready for glory and a few rundown buildings that only speak of past glory. The hogs are gone, but not the 'homilies'. Tucked away in my memory are the spiritual sermons that shaped my life.

Introduction

I just celebrated my 58th spiritual birthday and the foundation of my faith was well-established on that rock-infested homestead in Northern Maine. A few years ago I wrote down my thoughts to explain where my theological beliefs were established:

> "I have but a simple country creed, a terrain theology, a 'dirt' doctrine, a farm faith! Years ago, in my barnyard boyhood, I decided to stake all that I am or ever hope to be on the teachings of a country carpenter from Galilee. Though I left the Blackstone homestead over forty-five years ago, I still live in its fragrance and faith. When Jesus strolled the back lanes of Judea, He taught through trees and birds and seeds. Perhaps this is why I picked up His philosophy so quickly in my youth. The more I read through His theology, the more I could relate to it through my surroundings on the homestead. When He talked of the sower going forth to sow his seeds, I could see my grandfather and my father doing the same thing. When He spoke of the sparrow and its fall, I too watched as the little bird tumbled from the hayloft to the barn floor. When He taught of the trees and their significance to the kingdom, I understood the meaning of the forest because I lived in one. I did and still don't understand everything the Man from Galilee was saying, but I did and do understand His object lessons from my days of walking in the hills and living in the hallows of the homestead. In the complexity of sunlight and shadows, I saw in the darkness of a walk through the cow barn at night just how black sin can be in the human heart, but I also discovered in the light of the midday, homestead sun, just how brilliant the glory of the Lord can be. As I grew, the pasture parables of sheep and shepherds became for me the same as herds of Holsteins and herdsmen (Yes, I was a cow-boy!). Sheep were replaced by cows. When 'green pastures' and 'still waters' were mentioned my mind's eye immediately viewed the Russell Place with its ponds and creeks in pastureland of green fields (I know now after visiting Israel I had a wrong concept of David's psalm, but for a farmhand from Maine the point was clearly seen: God will provided for his own whether Palestine or Perham). The longer I live the more I am convinced

Introduction

that my real seminary training began long before I went off to Bible school in Greenville, South Carolina. In my boyhood, I spent most of my free days outdoors; whether working in the fields, or playing in the forest, I was constantly faced with reality. Life and death was a normal part of life. Long before my first funeral, I had looked death in the eye and learned it was nothing to fear, or be afraid of; whether feline or friend, death was just part of life and living. I also learned that the simple pleasures of life were much more rewarding than the worldly passions of excess. To pick dandelions in the spring, and to listen to the songbirds in the summer were much more pleasurable than picking up friends and going to the movies. A walk alone along the fence line was far more joyful than a walk through the red light district. I have come to the city now to pastor, but my creed is still well-established in the lessons I learned from the land as a lad and the teaching from the trees I learned from my teens. *I preach today an outdoor kind of faith to an indoor kind of world.* It's time we as a society retrace the steps of the Master, and learn His country creed and conduct!"

It is for these and other reasons that I compile for you this group of 'homestead homilies'. I would like, if only in my mind, take you back to a time where sermons were preached while mucking out the cows and picking potatoes. I want you to know of Read, Addie, Carroll, Glenna, Phyllis, Maude, Joyce, Clayton, and Wendell before you meet them in Heaven. I want you to see that in the greatness of the Creation, the Eternal Creator can teach you outside the church sanctuary as well as in it; that if you would pay attention these words from Job, pointed out to me by my father in my childhood, are still in effect today: *"But ask now the beasts, and they shall teach thee; and the fowl of the air, and they shall tell thee; or speak to the earth, and it shall teach thee: and the fish of the sea shall declare unto thee. Who knoweth not in all these that the hand of the Lord hath wrought this? In whose hand is the soul of every living thing, and the breath of all mankind."* (Job 12:7–12) I didn't realize it then, but I understand it now that I was taught from an early age this precept by Job and another written by Paul

INTRODUCTION

to a young man named Timothy: ". . . . *let them learn first* to shew piety at HOME. . . . " (I Timothy 5:4) May these 'homestead homilies' take you back HOME, to a place where you too first heard a soil sermon and were taught a land lesson; where your farm faith was developed. Even if you never lived on a homestead, it is my prayer that these 'homestead homilies' will challenge you to seek the Man from Galilee, a country preacher who came not only to teach you how to live, but to give you real life through His death on a tree on a hill!

Barry Blackstone

1

Plowing Straight

R. W. COOPER REMINDED me today of a place and a plowman from my past. The poem entitled, *'Plowing Straight'* goes like this: *"I remember as a youngster, when my father said to me, looking backward down the furrow, and then right down at me, always plow as straight a furrow as it's possible to do; men will judge you by your plowing when they think of hiring you. If your furrow row is crooked and you don't plow deep and true, they'll know you're not a worker for the task they want to do. What a practical philosophy, I suspect it can't be beat. Whether work or life or morals, let's keep those furrows neat!"* Such was the instruction given to me on the day my father Wendell took me to the backside of the Blackstone homestead and taught me the proper way to plow and I see now to live!

It was late October as I jumped on the Old John Deere tractor and followed Dad to the Paul Place. The woods were void of color as we worked our way through the field road that lead to a hilly section of the farm named after the family that once owned the property. The fallen fall foliage carpeted our path as we turned onto the ten acre field on the side hill. The land had yielded its increase of oats and straw, but to prepare it for a spring planting of Katahdins (the only variety of potato we grew in my childhood), it had to be plowed. The sounds of autumn were everywhere as Dad got off the red Massy-Ferguson tractor and got on the green John Deere with me. Explaining the ins and outs of a three-bottom plow, we headed down across the field. He showed me the proper speed of the tractor, the proper depth of the plowshare, and the proper vision and goal located on the far edge of the field. *"Looking back, looking around, or looking down was the worst thing I could do,"* said Dad. Father was a farmer who loved a straight row, whether a potato row, a furrow, or a beau.

After a few practice runs, Dad got back on his tractor with a four-bottom plow behind, and we began plowing the field together. Soon however the newness of the autumn adventure began to wear off on the rookie plowman. I became distracted by the warm 'Indian summer' day developing, and instead of focusing on my plowing I began to look around. I heard a honking overhead and upward I stared as a V-shape flight of wild Canadian geese passed overhead heading south. My momentary diversion was mirrored in the furrow. As I neared the end of the field near the woods, a pair of bushy-tailed, bright-eyed squirrels busily gathering their winter's stores caught my attention as I looked away. Again that furrow wasn't as crisp and clean as some of the others. As the morning stretched into afternoon, I began to notice the difference between my furrows and Dads. His were all straight and true to the goal. Mine on the other hand had waves and sections unplowed where my wandering eye had tempted me away from my course.

In forty plus years of being a pastor, I have made the observation that life is a lot like plowing. If people do not *'press on toward the goal for the prize of the upward call of God in Christ Jesus'*, (Philippians 3:13 RS) they will leave a lot of crooked rows behind them. Jesus Himself said: *"No man, having put his hand to the plough, and looking back, is fit for the Kingdom of God."* (Luke 9:62) A lesson I first learned one autumn day from a Paul Place plowman turned preacher. A true "homestead homily" that has affected my life and governed my life for much of my life!

2

Creation's Groan

I READ ONCE OF two travellers who were camping on the edge of a great desert. At midnight one was aroused by his companion asking, "What is that moaning sound I hear?" His traveling comrade replied, "That is the desert sighing!" I am hearing that same sigh from my ancestral home in Northern Maine. Can land lament? Can soil sigh? Can ground groan?

I have studied to long (47 year now a serious student of the Word) the Holy Bible not to know these words from the pen of Paul, *"The whole creation groaneth and travaileth in pain together until now."* (Romans 8:22) I have walked to long in the natural world not to detect the sighs and groans of this planet in relationship to what man is doing to the land and the ocean and the atmosphere. I might live four hours and two hundred miles from my hallowed homestead, but I lived to long on that sacred sod not to know of its aches and pains now. I feel like Goethe who wrote, *"Often have I had the sensation as if nature in wailing sadness entreated something to me, so that not to understand what was longed for cutteth to my heart."* I am also cut to my soul by the sound of the soil as man 'progresseth' passed my 'pasturable' (my word) paradise. Ground being neglected and rejected because man thinks its usefulness and fruitfulness is over as a productive dairy farm. I am neither a neurotic nor morbid, but I think the farm loved the fifties, and the soil loved the sixties (twentieth century). Those were the decades I lived on the homestead when I sensed only harmony and happiness between farm and farmer and farmhand. They were difficult years, but they were years when the land was still tilled by loving, caring hands. When the soil was still respected for what it could produce and provide for the good of mankind. I remember now the countless days we coddled the land. We gleaned the rocks from her back by hand. We hoed her potato rows by hand. We picked her bounty by hand. We spent plenty of time close to her heart, and she loved it. For most of us she knew we were just passing through, but she loved the attention we gave her while we were living with her.

Don't get me wrong, for I am not griping or grumbling or growling at those who have been forced by outsiders to farm differently, sell out to a modern way, but not necessarily a better way. Sure it was hard. Sure we ended the day dog tired. Sure we only made a living at best. Sure. . . . Sure. . . . Sure. . . . But think back with me, and remember what you heard from your homestead then, and compare it to what you hear now. Listen to the unutterable groaning's coming from cow less clover fields, barren barns, and fruitless forests; the 'amber waves of grain' are gone. The great stands of timber are gone; we will never hear again the sound they made when the autumn winds would blow heavily through their branches on a gusty day. The great herds of Holsteins are gone; we will never hear the music of moos echoing down the Russell Place valley by the milking shed on a foggy summer's day. The glorious haunting sounds of the homestead have been replaced by groaning. My beloved barnyard is now just another name on the casualty list of creation's castaways; that is until the great Creator, the Lord Jesus Christ, returns and once again restores the harmony of sod and soil, animals and mammals, creation and Creator (Isaiah 11:6–9). (Postscript: little did I know when I wrote this nearly a decade ago that I wouldn't have to wait for the millennial kingdom to hear these sounds again. At the publishing of this book my brother and cousin have sold the homestead to two Amish families that have restored the herds of cows and the way of life I remember!)

It is amazing to me that after all these years the farm is still preaching to me; still teaching me another Biblical lesson; that it still has another homestead homily to share, as it did last week when I returned to see how it was doing.

3

Dawn's Dawning

IT WAS THE OLD saga Job who lamented, "*When I lie down, I say, when shall I arise and the night be gone? And I am full of tossings to and fro unto the dawning of the day.*" (Job 7:4) I will be the first to admit that mornings are not my best times, but there is one part of the *"forenoon"* (my grandfather's word for morning) I do like: the dawn. In this age of fast, faster, and the fastest there is still one thing mankind has not been able to hurry-up: the dawning of a new day. Some wish they could, and other, like city-dwellers, try by their artificial lights to keep it daytime throughout the nighttime, but no matter, for it will dawn only when God's eternal clock says it's time to start a new day. Even man's new atomic clock can't be changed to speedup time; dawn's dawning will be neither be too fast or too slow!

When you lived the bulk of your childhood on a working potato and dairy farm you had ample opportunities to witness the glorious splendor of the birth of a morning. Few today take the time to watch darkness turn into day. Most would say, "I've seen that before." Whether through the old milking shed door carrying milk to the milk cans on the old '47 International pickup, or riding on the John Deere tractor into the back forty doing some early morning field work, the early light from the eastern sky was awe inspiring every time. And as God takes time beginning each and every new day on this planet, I learned in a Perham, Maine dawning, so should I! It still takes time for me to wake up after I get up. Even my dear wife Coleen has learned not to communicate with me before noon, for like the dawn I slowly come into the world.

Despite the season, or setting our clocks ahead in the spring or back in the fall, nothing has ever changed nature's wake up call. We rush through it; we can try to hurry it; we can speed up our lives with instant this and that, but no matter, the dawn will keep to its deliberate, delicate, and determined timetable no matter what we do or try.

This attempt by man to hurry the dawn is only a sign of a deeper problem facing him. It is the root transgressions of discontentment and impatience. We hurry through breakfast thinking lunch will be better, and surely we are late for work. I don't even waste my time to eat in the morning; I'd rather feast on the dawning pleasures of a new day. We hurry through a marriage thinking the next one will certainly be greater. My wife and I just celebrated 43 years (my parents 67, it is possible to live with one wife all your life), and we feel that we are still in the wonderful dawning of our relationship, for all of eternity is still before us. We hurry up our children's childhood only to make them as Vance Havner said, *"Precocious kids-all vine and no roots."* My children are in their thirties now, and my daughter just got marriage for the first time after waiting 34 years for the right guy, and my son is still looking for the right girl; he seems to be in no hurry. We often tear open the cocoon to soon in so many areas of our children's lives only to reveal a dead butterfly; beautiful, but dead. Morning and marriage and Marnie (that is my daughter's name) take time to unfold and develop, and only we have the means and choice to let them mature at God's pace. In the rat race that is today, we fail to realize that *"timing really is everything"* whether dawns or daughters, whether mornings or marriages!

Ever since that early morning sermon on the family farm, I have tried to let my life progress at its own pace, seeking God's face, not mine, or anybody else's. Now as I look back sixty-five years, it has made for some spectacular sunrises in my life!

4

Sad Succourer

MAUDE THOUGHT SHE NEVER accomplished much in her life!

She was always a very busy lady. Her husband had died in 1958 leaving her with over thirty-five years of widowhood. Maude use to share with me that she hadn't been much of a Christian when I would visit her in a small trailer on the side lawn of my parent's home. Her early days after Roy's departure was spent in a candy shop trying to make ends meet. Her six children had all married by this time, but that didn't make life any easier for Maude. Even when she had retired to live out her old age on the Blackstone homestead, her fervent spirit for work keep her busy right up to her final days on this planet. There was food to prepare for that hungry neighbor; there were mittens to knit for the needy children of the neighborhood; there were molasses cookies to bake for that grandson in a Bible school in the south (that was me); there were bandages to wrap for the missionary box going to Africa from the local Baptist church; there were birthday cards and anniversary cards to address to the great grandchildren, grandchildren and the children that lived far and near, and of course there were all those five dollar checks that had to be made out to put inside all those cards. There were flowers that had to be planted by her trailer and tended throughout the seasons so there would be a fresh bouquet on the communion table on Sunday morning. There were letters to be written to a countless group of friends and family that lived away. Maude was busy doing all sorts of things, not for reward or to be seen as over religious, but simply because she loved people and she liked meeting the needs of people whenever and wherever she could.

One day Maude fell sick, and the shadow of death gathered around her fail 94-year-old body. As in life she struggled for life, but after a long heroic fight she passed away into glory to meet her Saviour face to face and reunited with her dear husband. As she began that first walk along the streets of gold with her Lord on one side and Roy on the other things so darkly strange on earth became crystal clear in the celestial light. She apologized for not being much of a Christian during her earthly pilgrimage, explaining she just seem to be too busy to do much for her Master. To which Jesus reply, "What are you talking about?" "Oh, you know," answered Maude, "My never having enough time for you!" "For me," replied Jesus, "Why you always had time for me!" "I did," asked Maude, "When?" Then Jesus went on to explain, "You mean you didn't remember all those meals you cooked for me when I was so hungry; or all those colorful mittens you use to knit for me each winter to keep my hands warm; or those special batches of molasses cookies you use to bake for me when I was away from home; or all those bandages you wrapped to cover my sores when I was in such need for a little comfort; or all those birthday cards you sent me on my birthday with your last mite in each; or all those flowers you grew so my house would both smell good and look good on my day, and what about all those countless letters you wrote to me to keep in touch. What do you mean you never had any time for me, you gave all your time for me?"

It was then that Maude finally remembered the words of her Saviour that she often read in her well-worn Bible but never understood: *"Verity I say unto you, inasmuch as you have done it unto one of the least of these my brethren, ye have done it unto me."* (Matthew 25:40) Only then did my grandmother know what a sermon she had preached by her life, and what a homily she left behind to her family and friends, including her first-born grandson!

5

Grandmother's Help

MUM AND DAD CAME for a visit over the weekend to celebrate my son Scott's birthday. As we caught up on the news of the family from the county, an event from my boyhood came to mind in a conversation concerning my nephew Justin. I must admit I never remembered the event even after my mother told the story. Because it is too good a family homily to forget again, I will write it down for those who might get as much out of it as I did and the spiritual lesson it teaches!

Mother told me that this piece of my past happened when I was around four or five. It was autumn and the potato harvest was in full swing on the family farm in Perham, Maine. My sister Sylvia and I were still too small (by the time we were in the first grade we too were picking potatoes in the annual harvest) to participate in 'spud' (what we called potatoes) season, so we were staying with our grandmother Blackstone during the day while mother and father worked out in the potato fields. My sister and I had a wonderful relationship as children according to mother, and still do as adults. I am told that we played very well together and not a fight was remembered, or recalled. It seems on this particular day we were playing behind our grandparent's home in a rather large (at least to a small kid it was big) apple orchard. In those days, days without television, computers, or other gadgets, we pretty much had to make up our own games, entertain ourselves. The source, according to mother, of our adventures often led us to the stories of the Bible. Being brought up in a rural Baptist church, we heard all the famous Bible tales from our youngest years. Lily Harris was

9

our Children's Church teacher, and she loved to teach us through simple choruses which highlighted one of these Scriptural stories. On this day in the backyard of Grammy's house, we must have been thinking of that children's chorus that goes: *"Zacchaeus was a wee little man; a wee little man was he. He climbed up in a sycamore tree for the Lord he wanted to see. And as the Saviour passed that way he looked up in the tree, and said, 'Zacchaeus you come down, for I'm going to your house today!'"*

Who came up with the idea to reenact Zacchaeus mother never said, but I suspect Sylvia did. (She will probably tell the story differently.) As Mum tells the story, I played the part of Zacchaeus and Sylvia played the part of Jesus. Climbing up into a nearby crab apple tree which stood in for a sycamore tree (no sycamore trees in Aroostook County), I took my place on a low branch to wait the arrival of Jesus. My sister by that time had walked away from the tree to make her grand entrance. As she strolled up to the tree where I was setting, she repeated Jesus' famous lines, *"Zacchaeus, you come down, for I'm going to your house today!"* (Luke 19:5) What happened next, nobody, including myself, seems to know or remember? Sylvia again and again shouted the instructions that should have gotten Zacchaeus out of the tree, but I was seemingly frozen scared in the old crab apple tree. After Sylvia's cries went unheeded, she ran into the house to get grandmother. Upon reaching Grammy she is reported to have announced, *"Zacchaeus won't come down out of the sycamore tree!"*

I was rescued that day by my Grammy Glenna from the clutches of my imaginary sycamore tree. I don't remember the feeling of those warm and caring arms engulfing me, but I no doubt was thankful for the help; when like Zacchaeus I was 'up a tree and out on a limb' with no hope except for a helping hand. Over the years I have been found in similar situations and the Good Lord has always had someone there to help, have you?

6

Morning Song

ALTHOUGH I LIVE IN the middle of a city, I go to bed each night in the spring and the summer and the fall with my window open. (only in the coldest winter nights do we shut our bedroom window) This is not only for the cool air that filters in that makes sleeping in a city tolerable, but for the music of the morning. For as I doze in and out of sleep in the predawn hours of the day, the song of the morning birds brings me gently into the world of the living; remember, morning isn't my best part of the day. An a cappella bird quartet might seem out of place in a bustling city like Ellsworth, Maine, but it is one of the similarities with my Blackstone homestead in Perham, Maine. To this day with my eyes closes and my ears opened, I often wonder whether I'm in a city or the country. An old Hebrew prophet put it best when he wrote centuries ago: *"From the uttermost part of the earth have we heard songs!"* (Isaiah 24:16) And the city has always been an 'uttermost' place for me!

Sometimes in the morning I slip into a dreamland as my memory goes back four decades and more, and I'm a boy again getting up in the country. After a hard day's work, I went to bed at a decent hour and went to sleep unaided. No pills were needed in those days, just *"now I lay me down to sleep, I pray the Lord my soul to keep. If I should die before I wake. I pray the Lord my soul to take!"* After a God-given rest that was so necessary on a hard working farm was finished, I would be awakened by birds not buzzers, by songs not sirens, by robins no radios! The morning song of a bird outside my open bedroom window was the only motivation I needed to get my heart pumping, my feet moving, my soul restored, and my mind activated again.

This old world has gotten a lot nosier since this country boy last woke on the farm to the hymns of the homestead. Yet in all the holocaust of sound that has polluted this old world, the music of whoo-oo, hoo-oo, hoo of the morning dove; the squeaks, whistles, and clicks of the starling; the oh-ka-lee, oh-ka-lee of the blackbird; the chink, chink of the grosbeak; the twee-twee-twee of the warbler; the see-lip, see-lip, see-lip of the robin; the slip-lip, tsit-tsit of the shallow; the chrip, cheep of the sparrow; the zeee, zeee, zeee of the finch, and the chick-a-dee-dee-dee of the chickadee reminds me that even in the world's attempts to shut them off or block them out, some things haven't changed, even if they live in a city. Vance Havner once wrote, *"And what hasn't changed is far more important than what has changed."* The birds I know have never changed their tune!

I have come to believe that the reason most people get so stressed out today is they don't take time to listen to God's morning chorus that can calms the soul and clears the mind. Instead of a blessing most opt for a blast of rock-and-roll. An hour spent with nature's top ten birds would do us more good than with America's Top Forty. What we need is to give up a few minutes in the morning to creation's choir, lest we give up our sanity to the sounds that can only wind us up rather than winding us down. Even the song of a single swallow at a still, spring sunrise can go a long way towards restoring a stressful soul. When will we realize that what we need to start each day is just outside our window: a singing sermon? So tomorrow, why don't you open your window before you open the door and listen for a few minutes to the music of the morning? I didn't realize it then but I am thankful for it now that my father taught me to listen to the birds in the morning before listening to him; because '. . . . the fowls of the air, and they shall tell thee. . . . " (Job 12:7) We can learn a lot through their sweet sounds and spiritual songs!

7

Sacred Sanctury

I HAVE JUST RETURNED from a walk to my sanctuary in Ellsworth, Maine. I am not talking of a room in the church building from where I am the pastor of the Emmanuel Baptist Church, but a tranquil place out in God's creation were a soul can find peace and quiet and commune with his Maker. Every place I have lived in my earthly pilgrimage I have found such a sanctuary. In my first pastorate in Pembroke, New Hampshire, it was a small knoll overlooking Bear Brook State Park called Catamount Hill. During my stay in Westfield, Maine while pastoring Calvary Baptist Church, it was a small private trout pond called Smith Hole. When I moved my family to Moose Island off the Downeast coast of Maine to Eastport, I found Shackerford's Head a fitting sanctuary. Now that I live in Ellsworth, it is the Old Mills Highway. It is a side road into Ellsworth which follows the Union River by Leonard's Lake. It is an untypical country lane in a coastal city, but a wonderful place to walk and unwind, to pause and meditate. One particular spot is extremely serene, that being where a bridge, long since demolished, use to cross the small river. But no matter how far I roam, or how many sanctuaries I find traveling through this noisy world, none will ever compare to my first sanctuary on the Blackstone homestead in Perham, Maine.

The old homestead still stands in the Northern Maine Woods. The old rambling farmhouse I was raised in still invokes great memories despite the fact my folks no longer live there. If they taught me anything in my twenty-two years living under their roof, it was to find a place to reflect, to rewind, and to talk with

God. The Psalmist put it best when he wrote, *"To see Thy power and Thy glory, so as I have seen Thee in the sanctuary."* (Psalms 63:2) Nobody ever gets inspired in a chair watching television, that usually only winds you up, and rarely calms you down. We are living in a world that Ernest Hemingway once described as "The Millennium of the Untalented"! We are surrounded with writers with no imagination, farmers who can't farm because it is more profitable to take government subsidies, actors who can't act, preachers who don't preach the Word, singers who have no meaningful songs to sing, and leaders who can't inspire because they are not inspired except to keep their jobs! What we all need is a sanctuary; a place to come aside before we come apart, and in my earliest years I searched the homestead up and down for one spot of my own. I still remember the first time I stepped foot on its sacred sod. I was twelve and in love, or so I thought at the time. It was what we use to call 'puppy love', but at twelve I was smitten. The love of my life had dumped me for a classmate, and I was devastated. When I got home from the longest day I had ever spent in school (the rejection took place during morning recess) I went for a long walk down the Salmon Lake Road just below my home. I walked its length until I came to a small hill overlooking the lake. As I took in the wonderful sight before me a peace and serenity I had never experienced before filled my soul and calmed my spirit. I had found a place where distractions were blotted out (even though I could see my ex-girlfriend's house beyond the lake), and comfort was everywhere, which included the truth that 'this too would pass away' and another girl would come into my life!

When God created the first man and woman He didn't put them in a city, but a garden. I have, for most of my life, thought that a significant action of God. We all need a sacred sanctuary where we can get a fresh look at life, hear from God, and move on with our lives. Man created cities (Genesis 4:17), only God can create an Eden. Do you have one?

8

Weathering Weather

IN MY YEARS IN Maine and elsewhere, including India, I have observed the sudden and often dramatic changes in the weather. The old saying of "If you don't like the weather in Maine, just wait awhile and you will" is true! From my many years on the homestead in Northern Maine to my even more years on the coast of Downeast Maine, I have come to the conclusion that we have a lot to learn about life from the weather.

The Preacher of Ecclesiastes once shared with his readers, "He that observeth the wind shall not sow; and he that regardeth the clouds shall not reap." (Ecclesiastes 11:4) I witnessed these concepts being lived out long before I read this verse in the Bible. Each morning I rose on a family potato and dairy farm in Perham, Maine the weather wasn't always corporative with the work of the day. Grandpa and Dad never waited for ideal weather to farm, but they watched carefully the weather to know when best to farm. To plant the potato crop in ground still cold from winter's frost was just as bad as not planting at all. To harvest the potatoes in a damp fall rain was more harmful to the crop than leaving them in the ground for a few more days. I learned early that the weather was a key ingredient in the day in and day out operation of the Blackstone homestead, whether crops or cows, and as I would learn later Christians as well!

What I found true of the winds and weather in the barnyard, I found true in the conditions that surround the believer. Most believers desire only mountaintop experiences in fair winds and clear skies. Most seem to be totally unprepared for life's changing climate. An unexpected gust, or a breeze that catches them off-guard and they tumble into the drab and dismal valley below where the weather is anything but pleasant or ideal. Some seem to feel that when they got saved they would forever live in a world where a bird forever sings and a cloud will never spoil a sunny day. For any of us who have travelled this road of life very far know this is a 'pie-in-the-sky' idea pedaled by a string of 'positive-thinkers' who haven't a clue what life is all about from the perceptive of God's Word. This is why the Bible encourages us to watch the weather. Jesus once made reference to the weather: *"When it is evening, ye say, it will be fair weather: for the sky is red. And in the morning, it will be foul weather today: for the sky is red and lowering. O ye hypocrites, ye can discern the face of the sky; but can ye not discern the signs of the times?"* (Matthew 16:2–3) You know weather but do you know the Word?

There will always be uncertainties and puzzling questions about life, yes, even your life! Doubts will assail like a winter 'nor'easter' (I was born in a classic Maine nor'easter in 1951, perhaps, that is why life has never been as difficult for me as some!) and contradictions in logic will cause us to struggle with life even to unsettling us as with the changing of the seasons (Like recently when we discovered our 39 year old son Scott was dying with stage 4 lung cancer!). But as with the dramatic swing of the seasons we can remain calm if we are properly resting in the arms of our Lord and Saviour Jesus Christ. We might be blown about outside, but in Christ we will not waver. Paul put it this way in a letter to the Church at Corinth: *". . . but we were troubled on every side; without were fightings, within were fears. Nevertheless God, that comforteth those that are cast down, comforted us . . . "* (II Corinthians 7:5–6) For all the storms I have seen rock the countryside and the coastline, I have yet to see a storm blow either away. So it is with the Christian, *"I will,"* said Jesus, *"liken him unto a wise man, which built his house upon a rock: and the rain descended, and the floods came, and the winds blew, and beat upon that house; and it fell not: for it was founded upon a rock!"* (Matthew 7:24–25) I have, but have you?

9

Plodding Plodder

JAMES RUSSELL LOWELL'S FAMOUS lines came to me today as I watched the sixth snowstorm of the season blanket Ellsworth, Maine with over a half foot of fresh snow:

> The snow had begun in the gloaming,
> And busily all the night
> Had been heaping field and highway
> With a silence deep and white.
> Every pine and fir and hemlock
> Wore ermine too dear for an earl;
> And the poorest twig on the elm-tree
> Was ridged inch-deep with pearl.

It was in the snowstorms of Aroostook County, the snow banks of Perham, Maine and the snowdrifts of the Blackstone Homestead I first learned the importance of plodding.

How I love to tramp through newly fallen snow! I am nearly sixty-six, but a snowstorm is still an exciting event of the first importance to me. Ever since my early days on the family farm, when I loved to see the snow come so I wouldn't have to go to school, I have cherished each 'nor'easter' in turn. Yesterday's storm of yesteryear closed the kid's school, but as they slept in, I was up walking in the white stuff. A snow sanctuary fit for the angels of heaven greeted me as I crossed the street in front of the parsonage and waded through the drifts between the neighbor's house and the church on the other side of the road. Because of the freezing rainstorm a few days before, the highway was slippery under the snow, so I had to be extra careful. Plodding along, I pondered the countless times I walked through the snows of my boyhood.

Sometimes, a storm would drop a foot or two of snow on the fields and forests surrounding the old rambling farmhouse I called home for 22 years. Add a gusty breeze and the snowy landscape was often three to four feet deep. Running was impossible, and walking was difficult, but plodding could get you anywhere. One of my favorite spots to plod was to a spruce grove behind our massive cow barn. The combination of white, green, and blue in a mid-winter's afternoon was inspiring and impressive. The sturdy spires of spruce topped with a snow-woven design of white was thrilling to see, and the only way to get up close and personal was by plodding foot by foot through the deep snow, one deliberate step at a time. Up and down, up and down one leg at a time, each stride taking you a few more inches through heaven's treasure. It was many years after this plodding I found this question in God's Bible: *"Hast thou entered into the treasures of the snow?"* (Job 38:22) Finally, when I arrived at my destination and stood silently under a canopy of evergreen and white, knee deep in crystalized water, the peaceful snowbirds began to sing. One can only come to such a tranquil place by plodding! The Apostle Paul's words for plodding were "all perseverance". (Ephesians 6:18) Not fast, not slow, but a consistent stride is necessary to be a plodder in walking through snow or walking through life. Whether a walk, or a work, one must plod on until the task is finished, and the race is run; remember, a marathon, not a sprint! Vance Havner once wrote, *"God values more the plodding soul who stays with it patiently day in and out then the excitable brother who indulges in occasional outbursts of rapture."*

10

Country Calm

I HAVE JUST FINISHED a book by the world famous preacher, Charles R. Swindoll, (a man I got the privilege to meet in his church in Texas when my daughter was attending a seminary nearby, a school Swindoll used to be the president of, Dallas Theological Seminary) in which he talked about the stressful society we are now living in. Often I am asked about stress, but I know little about what they speak. Even after I read countless medical and mental definitions of the word I still have a hard time relating to it. Why, you may ask? To which I humbly reply, "I have known little of stress because I was raised and taught very early in my life about 'country calm.'" The Psalmist says of God, "He maketh the storm a calm, so that the waves thereof are still." (Psalms 107:29)

I was brought up on an old-fashion potato and dairy farm in a country county of Maine. Despite the hustle and bustle of a busy barnyard, it was and still is the quietest and most tranquil place I have ever lived. I was raised on walks along babbling brooks, and peaceful pathways of calm. I was reared on still strolls through melodious meadows, and fabulous fields of calmness. I was the recipient of a life and a lifestyle that highlighted and underlined the value of 'Christian-calmness'. I use to ride my bike along country lanes that rarely saw a passenger car, or a person. I have just returned from visiting our nation's capital where I came the closest I can ever remember to a stress attack or as Chuck calls it *'a stress fracture'!* My wife said I had one, but knowing I was only passing through decided I would put off my first major stress attack to another day. I resisted the temptation to have 'a stress fracture' hoping I would soon be out of the madding race that is the Washington Beltway. The easy-going lifestyle of the family farm was just the tonic and teaching I needed to create in me a calm nature even in the midst of strife and stress. I was instructed through example how to remain calm even in the most critical circumstances or sobering situations.

I remember well the calm my father always exhibited throughout my years under his supervision. Despite the responsibilities of a big farm and family, a town office, and a church deaconship, Dad always seemed to remain perfectly calm. So very early in life I learned if father's in charge and is calm, why should I get excited when the manure spreader broke, or the Holstein cow stepped on my toe. Life will go on and does, so why make it worse by fretting and fussing about it; just keep pitching and hobble on and remain calm! There always seems to be those who would fuss and fume, but my father choose to walk another way, and to be honest from my earliest years to my latter years I have been able, most of the time, to follow the calming course demonstrated by my Dad (a man of 92 now)! Anxiety and anger were not a part of my father's vocabulary or emotions, so I tried not to make them mine either. *"This too shall pass away!"* Has been a motto of mine, and a saying my family has gotten tired of hearing me say, but it is my way of simply admonishing, "Relax, take it easy, stay calm, for this too shall pass away."

We live in the 'Aspirin Age' were 'calm' has become a four-letter word to most. Nobody is calm any more without help from a pill or two. If you are calm without some kind of medication, or acting calm in a crisis for some reason you will be criticized for being uncaring, unconcerned, or uncompassionate. I have taken such constructive criticism over the years and have placed every complaint and placed them all in the calm corner of my cranial. I was raised on country calm *"and the peace of God, which passeth all understanding, shall keep your hearts and minds through Christ Jesus."* (Philippians 4:7)

11

Peaceful Place

IF I WERE ASKED to summarize my childhood in one word, it would have to be the word: *peaceful*. Is there a rarer quality in this world today than peace? It is a virtue that has become more valuable than the desired diamond, or the rarest ruby. It has become a prize sought for by the most powerful, and the most poor, yet none has been able to attain unto it. It has become the pastime of the most skillful diplomats in the world, as well as the neighbor next door, but it remains an elusive goal. However, in an age long since passed, I found and experienced this wonderful tranquility and learned to "... *seek peace, and purse it."* (Psalms 34:14)

The Perham, Maine I knew in the 1950s and 1960s was a land at peace with itself and its inhabitants. I would even be so bold as to call it a place of perfect peace. Man and nature working and living hand in hand with each other. Oh, there was the occasional difference of opinion on the weather needed at a particular time, but the sun rose and sat daily and the early and the latter rains came on time, and the crops grew and the cows matured, and springtime and summertime and harvest time and wintertime past in perfect unity and in unison with each other. Year passed from year to year with no panic, only peace; month passed from month to month with no fearfulness, only peace, and day passed from day to day with no difficulty, only peace. Some might say I was living in a fantasy world unaffected by the problems that did exist in the world (remember this was the world of the Cuban Missile Crisis, the Vietnam War, civil unrest on the college campus, and the threat of an atomic apocalypse), but Shangri-La or no Shangri-La I knew my world, at least, was at peace. I knew peace when I felt it, faced it, and found it in my family or out in the middle of a field. Despite the odd fight with a cousin, or the odd conflict with a friend, I remember more days of peace than any other characteristic.

In the 3500 plus years of recorded human history wherein mankind has sought peace there has been few years of peace. According to the experts in this field only 286 of those years has the world seen a universal peace? Why is that? The answer for me is quite simple. Man's doesn't really want peace! There was peace on the family homestead because there were people who really wanted peace and were ready, willing and committed to paying the price for peace. Perham became a peaceful place to practice peace, and nobody should fool themselves into thinking that peace came easy; it must be worked at every day. Whether in my home on the Russell Place, or in my grandparent's house on the Blackstone Road, I recall very few fights, squabbles, or outbursts of anger. I was brought up in a tolerant, calm, relaxed environment: this despite cows dying, crops failing, and children aligning. I remember when the shocking word came that my youngest sister Lori would be a diabetic at six. I remember that calming breeze that stabilized our family after the initial shock. So amid uncertain futures on the price of potatoes, unfulfilled dreams of being a soldier in the United States Army, and the unpleasant circumstances surrounding Lori's health, there was one piece of the farm and family that stayed constant, and has stayed with me all these years, a doctrine of Perham Peace; a peace that I discovered at seven come through my family's belief in the Lord Jesus Christ. Spiritual faith translates into peace when you consider these words from the Lord of my family: *"Peace I leave with you, my peace I give unto you: not as the world giveth, give I unto you. Let not your heart be troubled, neither let it be afraid."* (John 14:27) We didn't then nor do I now allow anything to take away my peace; a peace that comes from only one source: *"And the peace of God, which passeth all understanding, shall keep your hearts and minds through Christ Jesus!"* (Philippians 4:7)

12

Blessed Hope

MY ANCESTRAL HOME IN Perham, Maine has witnessed enormous challenges since 1861. Despite the stress and strain of summer droughts and winter blizzards it remains (2016). Despite the pressure and pounding of spring rains and autumn snows it survived. With undaunted courage my forefathers have managed to keep stable a life and a lifestyle through seasons of illnesses, crop failures, financial reversals, domestic disappointments, and the death of a series of matriarchs and patriarchs for four generations (my dad and mum, the fifth, are both in their 90s). What is it that has kept alive the seven generations of Blackstones that now have lived on that corner of Aroostook County? One irreplaceable ingredient has and still abides and remains, "According to my earnest expectation and my *hope*. . . . " (Philippians 1:20)

The homestead has rebounded against wind and weather, calamity and catastrophe, disease and death, insects and isolation because of *hope*. For it learned very early in its existence that one can survive months without passable roads, weeks without rain, and days without the sun, but no house, home, or homestead can or will last very long without *hope*. Where there is no *hope*, you don't press on through a hot dry summer; without *hope*, you throw in the towel when half your year's wages rots in the potato ben, and with the absence of *hope*, you quit planning potatoes and you stop milking cows, and when you stop planting and milking there is no harvest, no milk and the farm stops, dies! *Hope* is the irreducible catalyst of determination, drive, and duty if you're a farmer. Unless a life is anchored to *hope* there is no joy of living, no happiness of life, and no peace of lifestyle. Unless the land and the lives on that land are bathed in *hope* there will be no harvests of any kind: crops, cows, or kids!

In some of my earliest remembrances, reflections of my family farm come to my memory and mind the reoccurrence of the word '*hope*.' I never realized it then, but as I ponder on the bites and pieces of past conversations with the inhabitants of the homestead that still rattle around in my brain I recall hearing such things as: "*Hope* it rains today; *hope* the wind comes up to dry the hay; *hope* the frost stays away for a few more days, so we can finish digging; *hope* the Vet finds out what is wrong with No. 68 (a cow); *hope* Lori feels better; *hope* the market is a bit higher next month; *hope* the potatoes hold up; *hope* the thunderstorm hasn't knocked down the oats." Now I see I lived in a refuge of *hope* around a people of *hope*. A place and a people who kept on *hoping* even when it didn't rain, the wind didn't blow, the frost did come early, old 68 died, Lori got worse, the market dropped, the potatoes turned to mush, and the storm leveled the oats!

If *hope* is the opposite of hopelessness, and I believe that it is; despite the hopelessness that often haunted the homestead, *hope* remained, and a few minutes walking on or wandering through that place, in mind or memory, still gives me *hope* that no matter what happens in my life I can still press on in *hope*. For with *hope* all things and anything is possible, no matter how hopeless the circumstance or the situation may seem (like terminal cancer). The homestead thrived on *hope*, and it wasn't long before I learned it wasn't *hope* in the land, but *hope* in the Lord! Only as I grew older in the Lord did I come to understand this doctrine on *hope*: "*For we are saved by hope: but hope that is seen is not hope: for what a man seeth, why doth he yet hope for? But if we hope for that we see not, then do we with patience wait for it.*" (Romans 8:24–25) So where does your *hope* lie? In your lands and your gold, or in "the blessed *Hope*" (Titus 2:13) that is Christ!

13

Farmer's Psalm

I HAVE ALWAYS BEEN interested in verse. I love 'good' poetry, not the stuff they pass on as proses today with no reason or rhyme to it. I feel the explanation for this love affair with poetry was my early introduction to the King James Version of the Holy Bible. Though many today despise the language of the old English, I for one have become a fan. While many of my fellow-pastors have abandoned the KJV, I am still preaching and teaching using it, despite the 50 years since my first sermon; too late to change now! Sure, it is difficult to read at times with all of its 'thee' and 'thou' and the changes in meaning of some of the words, but for me, its words flow gracefully and its language can paint wonderful word pictures like no other form of English. This is particularly visible in the book of the Bible called 'The Psalms', and the most famous of all the psalms: The Twenty-Third Psalm. One day as I pondered where David was when he composed this literary classic, I realized it could have just as well been a Blackstone homestead psalm, "But David went and returned from Saul to feed his father's sheep at Bethlehem." (I Samuel 17:15) In 2010 I had a chance to visit the fields outside of Bethlehem, and I was amazed at the similarity of the rolling hills and pasture fields between Bethlehem, Israel and my hometown of Perham, Maine.

    I have drawn much inspiration from my family's homestead as you have already noticed in these 'homestead homilies'. My meditations on the homestead, and my remembrance of David's inspiring lines (one of the first pieces of the Bible I committed to memory as a child) one day blended together. Because David's words have been rattling around my brain for decades it is not strange that one day the spirit of that immortal psalm and the feeling I have for the old homestead would come together. I would like to call this 'the farmer's 23rd psalm':

> The Lord is my supplier, I shall not want.
> He maketh me plant in dry fields.
> He leadeth me to sow the right crops.
> He restoreth my seed.
> He leadeth me in the way of conservation, for the farm's sake.
> Yes, though I go through a summer with little rain, I will fear no drought.
> For thou art with me.
> Thy sun and thy dew, they shower my fields and flocks.
> Thou prepareth a time of harvest in the presence of frost.
> Thou anointeth my land with productivity.
> My potato house and milk tank runneth over.
> (The Blackstone homestead was both a dairy and potato farm- no sheep!)
> Surely good harvests and healthy herds shall follow me all the days of my farming.
> And I will dwell on the homestead forever.

The Hebrew poet wrote these lines well over three millennium ago while watching his father's sheep on the back side of their homestead. I wrote these lines less than three years ago while thinking about my boyhood homestead. I doubt you will remember my psalm far beyond this reading, but if you have a place as David did and I have; where inspiration flows behind every stone, perhaps you too in time will pen your own psalm?

14

Vivacious View

I LOVE ANY PLACE that has a view. Perhaps that is why I have never, or never will enjoy the city: no view! As I look out the window of my study at the Emmanuel Baptist Church in Ellsworth, Maine, what do I see? I see man's creative hand all around me and the few places that reveal the hand of God are being cut down and paved over for new businesses and apartment complexes. For some, mankind's inventions and ingenuity are marvels to behold. I too at times have been fascinated with the technological advancements of the human race (like the new narrows bridge that links Verona Island with Prospect) in relationship to skyscrapers, airplane terminals, and baseball and football stadiums. A spring trip to Washington D.C. resulted in many 'wows' and 'oohs' from even my lips, but the view, where was the view? Man tries to create a 'million-dollar' view by spending a billion dollars, but God's 'billion-dollar' view rarely costs us anything, that is until man gets ahold of it! I love the exhortation of *"Go, view the land."* (Joshua 2:1)

Today fall arrived, and with it the autumn season of my year. Though I am stuck in a city, surrounded by a fifty-cent view, my mind's eye has already focused on the most vibrant view on this planet (my opinion of course, but I am partial). Fall brings potato harvest time to my family's farm in Perham, Maine. As I write this homily, my brother Jay and my cousin Gary and other members of my family are digging out the summer spuds. The fields they are now hauling potatoes from, I once helped haul potatoes from, and all the time we worked with a view! I am confided to a small study with high windows, and if it weren't for the fishing paraphernalia and the family pictures covering the walls, this place would be a prison. Right beside my desk is a floor to ceiling bookshelf and three shelves up is a picture my mother gave me of a fall view looking down from our homestead to Perham Village in the valley; and what a view! I envy my family at this time each year: the sweet smell of potato soil filling their lungs; the fabulous foliage of autumn filling their sights, the crisp, clean crops of autumn filling their days, and the cool, clear skies of a harvest moon filling their nights. Who would ever give up a job with a view? I have asked myself that question for years.

As I survey the homestead in my memory for its most spectacular sight, I go to the top of the hill on the Blackstone Road. It is the highest point of land on my hallowed homestead. From there you can see almost every piece of the farm my family has called home since the beginning of the Civil War between the North and the South. From that knoll the land drops off on all four sides. It was my wife's and my desire to build a log cabin on that ridge someday. Little did we know in time we would inherit my grandparent's home just under that ridgeline, so now I have but a short stroll to that vivacious view. A place to retire, a place to die, a place with a view! From that spot you can see the little white church in the dale where we were married. From that point of land you can see the heart of the homestead, the very first framed house built in Perham in the year 1861. From that location you can see the burial grounds were six generations of Blackstones are buried in a place they called "FairVIEW" Cemetery. Oh, in the distance, on a clear day, you can make out the cities of Caribou (13 miles away) and Presque Isle (20 miles away), but each fades into nothingness as you view the multi-colored maples that dot the rolling hills surrounding that sacred soil. Autumn came today, and with it a longing to once again live in a place with a vista, with a view. I just know that the place the Good Lord is preparing for me in Heaven has a view! Don't you?

15

Perham Prayers

I HAVE JUST RETURNED to my study at the Emmanuel Baptist Church in Ellsworth, Maine after having a noontime lunch with my dear wife Coleen. As we bowed our heads for a short prayer of thankfulness before our food, a multitude of memories flashed across the screen of my mind; remembrances that I must jot down least I never think of them again. "For every creature of God is good, and nothing to be refused, if it be received with thanksgiving. For it is sanctified by the word of God and prayer." (I Timothy 4:4-5)

Grace is a long-standing family tradition in my home. I can't remember a mealtime grace wasn't offered up to the Almighty; potato house, farm house, grandparent's house, or the house of God. Whether the simple and short supplication of a five-year-old brother, or the elaborate and eloquent prayer of a pastor-uncle, all were meaningful and memorable on this day of remembrance. In this age of unprecedented wastefulness, I am disheartened by the times I live in because the only thing thought wasteful today is a few moments in prayer before a meal! We are a squanderous and spendthrift society in every way, yet we fail to see the value of a few minutes with our heads lowered and our hearts lifted to think and thank the Lord for His bountiful blessings. Words are so numerous today, they are cheap, and limitless, and yet, the only time we don't seem to use them is when we are about ready to eat. The printing presses grind out trillions of words daily, the air waves are loaded with talk show after talk show, and we can't pause for a second to talk to God who " . . . *giveth us this day our daily bread* . . . "

(Matthew 6:11). This is the way it is now, but I remember a day of 'grace', and I try to keep this instruction alive!

I first recall our daily family meals when dad would always lead in prayer; he saw it as his responsibility as well as a way to instill this practice in his five children. Dad was a man of few words, but he always had a few words of thanksgiving to say to his God before breakfast, before dinner, and before supper (for some it is lunch at noontime and dinner at supper time but not at the Blackstones). I have often thought that in my childhood father talked more to the heavenly Father than he did to me. A few words and the same words were often the pattern of my father's supplication before dining.

Then there were those Sunday night suppers (salmon sandwiches and oyster stew) at Grandpa and Gramie's house. On those Sundays when it was dad's turn to do the afternoon milking, we usually would have our evening meal with them just before we went back to the little white church in the vale for the evening service (another service that is no more). Grandpa would often lead in prayer, but sometimes he would ask someone else setting at the table. When I was young I would often take a peak to see what was happening. I still remember the seriousness and solemnness of the faces around the table as grace was offered. I learned early that prayer before a feast was important and instructive especially to a young believer, like myself (accepted Christ at the age of 7).

Other moments of grace I recall were the potato field prayers during the annual potato harvest. Depending who you eat with, the supplications could be quick and quiet, or long and length. I remember my cousin Doug as being shy in those days. If he were ask to pray you could hardly hear him. His older cousins would sometimes tease him, but if Uncle Read were nearby we would be reminded that God hears the prayer you can't, and besides, prayers are private and personal between the supplicator and the Saviour! When was the last time you took the time to say grace before a meal, in the home place or the public place? Another prayer time that has gone the way of the mid-week prayer meeting!

16

Family Preacher

As I ponder again my homestead home, it is a person not a place that comes to my memory and fond thoughts. Though he died many, many years ago, his signature on my life is still unerased and his impact on my ministry remains. He was Read Woodbury Blackstone, my favorite uncle, and the family preacher.

It was Uncle Read that brought faith back into the Blackstone family. Before Uncle Read, the Perham Blackstones had a lot to do with religion, but had very little to do with practicing Christ-like living. Uncle Read never intended to become a preacher when he got saved at the little Baptist Church in the village of Perham, Maine, but preach he did. For over forty-years, Read was the pastor of the Advent Christian Church of Dunntown; while at the same time farming in partnership with my grandfather Carroll. His was not your typical pastorate, yet he buried more people and married more people than most full-time, fully ordained ministers (seminary and formal Bible training). Most funerals and marriage ceremonies were scheduled around milking the cows and digging the potatoes. Often in my early years, I worked side by side with Uncle Read; whether shoveling manure off the bob shed in the winter, picking rocks in the spring, hoeing potatoes in the summer or unloading barrels of potatoes in the fall. It was then he got his text, outline, and illustrations for the next Sunday's sermon. How do I know? He'd share with me his thoughts long before Sunday morning arrived. Read was *a man of the cloth* who wore overalls!

I will always remember Uncle Read as the busiest man in the world who was never too busy for people, including his brother's grandson: despite, being a husband to Addie, a father to Clayton, Donald, Barnard, Wilma, and Lloyd, a grandfather to twenty grandchildren, a pastor to the same flock for 42 years, and a farmer of a 720 acre dairy and potato farm. If that wasn't enough, Uncle Read was a pioneer Christian radio broadcaster in Aroostook County, and held numerous special 'revival' meeting all over 'the county' (what we call Aroostook County-for us it is the only county in the state or country). Of these Read was best known for his services at the old Snowman Schoolhouse just outside the city of Caribou where Elmer Tompkins led the singing with his trumpet and Uncle Read did the preaching. Yet despite all these responsibilities, Read always took time to listen and encourage me in the things of our Saviour. I remember well the Monday after I preached (Commandments Christians Regularly Break) my first sermon (I was fifteen) at the First Baptist Church of Perham. Uncle Read got wind of it, and cornered me in the cow barn as I helped carry the milk from the milkers to the milk room. If I could preach at the Baptist Church then I could preach at the Advent Church in the next town. Two weeks later I was in his pulpit preaching my second sermon (Walking With God). Throughout the message all I remember was the "Amens" and "Hallelujahs" coming from Read's lips after seemingly every statement I made. He was also there bright and early every time I headed off to Bible school with a word of prayer for a safe trip. Needless to say, when it came time to marry, it was Uncle Read that performed the ceremony that not only joined Coleen Ardith Meister and Barry Alan Blackstone as one, but dedicated them both into the ministry. Uncle Read loved more than family and farming, he loved full-time Christian servants. Uncle Read, the family pastor and preacher taught me what Paul taught young Timothy long, long ago: *"If a man desire the office of a bishop, he desireth a good work."* (I Timothy 3:1)

17

Hallowed Hills

"I will lift up mine eyes unto the hills, from whence cometh my help."

(PSALMS 121:1)

HAVING BEEN RAISED IN the foothills and on the hillocks of Aroostook County, Maine, I know of the lure of the other side of the hill. I have hiked along many a hilly trail and the thrill is always around the next bend, around the next corner, around the next curve. It is like I like to call it *'the romance with anticipation and a love affair with expectation'!*

Anticipation and expectation are the true spirits of the other side of the hill. What we know, and have seen, often becomes dull and drab to us. Our daily path often loses its glamour and glitter as we repeat our walk, our daily routine, the same-old, same-old as I call it. The other side of the hill with its uncertainty and unexpected sights and sites draws us onward and often upward as we search for that illusive prize: something new! I have the same problem when I am fishing a meandering trout stream, or brook. The best hole must be just around the bend even when I'm standing in the best pool in the creek. I will always fish around one more corner before I head home, limit or no limit. Needless to say, this philosophy makes for some very long days on the river!

God has created our lives much like the hilly trail, the curving stream. How terrible would be our lives if it were just one long straight track? I remember in the summer of 1972 travelling on the straightest railroad track in the world at that time, and I dare say probably still to this day: three hundred miles of dead straight rails without a dip or a diversion to the right or to the left, and no detours. I was riding across the Gibson Desert in Western Australia with my cousin Bob. We were on a short-terms mission's trip to work among an Aboriginal tribe in a place called Warbunton Range. The train trip was the most boring time of our ten-week Australian adventure, and to top it off we had to retrace that section of travel on our way back home: can you say 'double-boring'! So is a life without its curves and bends and corners. We might not be able to see down the road, but that is what makes life the adventure that it is. We never know what is coming up, but we can know the One that knows.

Vance Havner has written, *"Indeed, that is what faith is: confidence in the One who knows the other side of the hill. We know so little of life, of truth, of God and destiny. Business crashes, health fails, friends depart, cherished dreams collapse-yet somehow. . . . most carry on. It is the other side of the hilly that does it."* Who of us hasn't thought to ourselves, "Well, next year will be better. Tomorrow will hold the answer. I'll feel better next month." All those thoughts are about the other side of the hill. So with our knapsack over our shoulder and a walking stick in our hand, we press on, push forward, and our goal: the other side of the hill, the other side of our problem, the other side of our dilemma. It may be a hill of pain, of lose, of uncertainty, of disappointment, but we just know once we are over it, or around it, there lies on the other side a glorious meadow, a babbling brook, a golden sunset that will change our lives.

For the Christian traveller however, there remains the last hill, the final bend, the ultimate corner. The world calls it death, but the Bible calls it a departure (II Timothy 4:6), the beginning of a life that will go on forever (John 3:16) in the presence of the God of the other side of the hill. A life where there will be no more corners, no more bends, no more curves because we will reach the end of our wandering, meandering journey at the feet of Jesus. Our strolling along the winding paths of earthly life will end on the other side of the hill in eternal life with Christ.

18

Blackstone Beekeeper

M. R. DeHaan once said, *"God's best schools have horizons for walls, a sky for a roof, and the earth for its floor!"* If this is true, and I believe it is, then I went to the best of schools in my boyhood: not Perham Elementary, not Washburn High School, not Bob Jones University, but Blackstone Homestead College.

Living as I did on the Blackstone homestead in Perham, Maine in the 1950s and 1960s, I enjoyed the benefits of nature's classroom, God's original classroom (Psalms 19:1–2). I was raised on home grown vegetables. I still like my vegetables fresh and raw! Fresh fruits were in abundance on the farm with plenty of fresh milk from our large Holstein herd of black and white cows. We had fresh eggs from our farm grown chickens which also supplied us with the occasional roast chicken dinner. We also had fresh meat from the cows and pigs raised on the homestead, and of course an ample supply of potatoes seeing we were a dairy/potato farm. And to sweeten the lot was our own bee's honey for toast and tea and a variety of other applications for the best taste in the world.

When I was in junior high school, we got a new pastor for our small country church in Perham village. What I remember best about this pastor, besides the fact he baptized me, was his hobby: he was a beekeeper. Pastor Cocky eventually got my father interested in his hobby, and it wasn't long before there were three bee hives setting beside the old potato house out behind our farmhouse. Dad became consumed with raising bees. He read magazines and books, and collected all the paraphernalia needed to develop a good string of bee hives that would produce an abundant supply of honey for our table and others. It was there in that open classroom I was tutored in the fine art of beekeeping. As Grandpa showed me firsthand how to prune the suckers from his prized apple trees and how to plant a straight row of carrots in his garden, Dad showed me how to tend the bees in his bee hives. Dad taught me how to spot a second queen bee forming in a hive (important for a second bee meant a split was about to happen that would weaken the hive and thereby produce less honey). Like the rogue stem on Grandpa's apple tree, the revival queen would divided the hive and take away valuable worker bees. If the hive was diminished and weakened its chances of surviving a long and sever Maine winter would be slim, if not impossible. Lessons I would see repeat themselves in my calling as pastor, for much like an apple orchard and a bee hive a pastorate too has it problems with rogue branches (John 15:2) and queen bees: the Bible calls them 'busybodies' (II Thessalonians 3:11). God is also looking for fruit and honey from his 'hive' and 'orchard' the church!

    I learned an even more valuable lesson one day as I accompanied my Dad to his bee hives. Because I had been careless in putting on my bee screen over my face, a bee got in. He buzzed in front of my face for a few minutes then attacked. He struck just under my left ear. I thought someone had hit me with a baseball bat. I ran back towards the house ripping the mask from off my face. The bee escaped and seemed to head back towards my face for another strike. Buzzing near my head, I hit the ground yelling. Dad was soon at my side with these comforting words, "The bee is now harmless. It cannot hurt you again. It has lost its sting." Dad then reached behind my ear and came back with the little black stinger between his fingers. Years after this memory came back to me, I recalled the words of Paul when he wrote, "O death, where is thy sting . . . the sting of death is sin." (I Corinthians 15:55–56) As with the bee, death will only get one shot at you and if you believe that Jesus took the sting of death away at Calvary then you have nothing to fear!

19

Chickadee Chorus

TODAY, I FILLED MY bird feeders for the first time since spring (summer in Maine provides the birds of Maine with ample feed, but with the coming of fall and the long hard winters Maine is known for I help the birds that remain in Maine-whereas must leave for southern destinations, the few that remain need plenty of help). Hanging from the limb of an old apple tree beside the parsonage of the Emmanuel Baptist Church in Ellsworth, Maine, the two feeding stations are full and awaiting the advent of autumn's final days and winter's snowy days: a blessed season of sound for me.

I have been an ardent bird listener since my early days on my parent's farm in Northern Maine. You notice I said listener, not watcher! Oh, I watch for birds, but my primary purpose for bringing birds to my feeders is to hear their psalms and hymns and songs. One day I hope to hear the seraph songs in Heaven, but until then I will hearken to the songsters of nature. I am still not very good when it comes to recognizing which bird is which, but that has not stopped me from enjoying the melodious music that comes from the songbirds that gather around my feeders each fall. In this day of ear-splitting noise they call music which bombards my eardrums from every side; I prefer the mellow music of the songbirds just like Jeremiah, the old Hebrews prophet, wrote: *"Behold their sitting down, and their rising up; I am their music."* (Lamentations 3:63) What a beautiful description of the birds that comes by my feeder!

Bird listening has taught me a valuable lesson about sacred music. Spiritual sounds don't have to be loud to be powerful; Oh, that the new generation of believers could learn this. Each time I hear one of those little songbirds whistle or chatter, I am instantaneously transported back to a simpler time and a solitary place. Being a product of a country setting has created in me a despising of anything loud and unnatural in music. Today where I live few people take the time to listen to the song sparrows as they spat over sunflower seeds. Even in their anger with each other, their tone is sweet and somber. Being raised near a large cow barn brought me many opportunities to witness the twitter chirp of the house sparrow or the creeping chimp of the song sparrow as they fought over space and supper. Often when I would go into the huge barn in the evening, I would find them sitting on the edge of the grain barrel. Instead of scaring them away, I would listen as they thanked their Maker and Master for such a place as the Blackstone homestead were food was filling and free. Oh that we would be as thankful (Matthew 6:25–30)!

It was not until I moved to the city that I discovered what a treasure I had on the homestead in the sounds of the swallows. It has become very difficult for me to entice many birds near the parsonage. The traffic and tenants of a close neighborhood don't provide the area for attracting too many birds, even hungry ones. So that is why I enjoy every note I hear from the few that perform outside my living room window. *A bird in a feeder is worth more than two in the bush.* So whether it is a chickadee choir or a grosbeak quartet either is a sweet sound to my ear. I can shut my eyes and hear the warbler's musical trill and know not whether I am in the city or the county?

I shall listen to these sporadic visitors to my bird feeders with an attentive ear because in the world that I live in it might be the only sensible sound I will hear that day. In this day of man-made music that often grieves the soul and quenches the spirit, the only sound that seemingly takes me back to God and my upbringing is the sweet hymn of the chickadee chorus by my bird feeder.

20

Farm Faith

I WAS REARED AND raised on the old-fashion, fundamental "faith of our fathers" (now there is a hymn)! However, that faith has almost gone the way of the dinosaur and doe-doe bird. Over my lifetime (65 years at this writing), we have spent so much energy and effort keeping the framework looking straight and sound, The Faith has nearly collapsed.

Bernard Shaw once observed, *"Americans have the best filing systems in the world, but no American can ever find a letter!"* The same is true with the average American Christian. We are so practical, having classified and cataloged Christianity to the point we have forgotten it is not a system, or a religion, but a way of life. We have built our church cathedrals and chapels to the glory of God, but have forgotten to invite Him into them, forgetting that He doesn't dwell in buildings but bodies (I Corinthians 3:16–17). We have forgotten that God and godliness can't be arranged into a ten-point plan for spiritual success, and five-minutes a day with God isn't enough! Just because we make the roll call on Sunday, doesn't guarantee we'll be saintly on Monday! The questions still remains, *"When the Roll is Call up Yonder, will you be there"* (Matthew 7:21–23)?

"The Faith of Our Fathers" is going the way of the Jewish faith. We have institutionalized Christianity to the point it is just another country club, social organization, or political party. We gather to map out our strategy for dealing with the social problems of our community, failing to even ask the Head of the Church to attend, or recognizing that until your change the soul you will never change society. We have done it our way for so long, thinking we know how to work it, we have forgotten the message delivered long ago by an old Hebrew prophet: *"For My thoughts are not your thoughts, neither are your ways My ways, saith the Lord."* (Isaiah 55:8) Vance Havner writes, *"You cannot organize religion. The very minute you take an emotion and try to make it into an institution, you'll kill it. When will we learn that we cannot preserve, propagate, and perpetuate any truth by organizing a club?"*

Getting back to "The Faith of Our Fathers" will mean tearing down the old structure that now hides "The Faith". It was the practical, day in, day out Christianity of my forefathers that drew me to "The Faith" in the first place. The Faith of Sunday at church lived out on Tuesday in the barn. The Faith that I witnessed on the Blackstone homestead of Northern Maine wasn't a Faith of creeds, ceremonies, or catechisms. We went to worship in a building in the hamlet of Perham, but the church paraphernalia wasn't the reason we went. As a matter of fact, it was a poor building then, but within its walls was a strong spiritual heartbeat that loved Christ and every Christian. The truth of Christ was spread through infection and influence, not some ideal of a better building, a better set of beliefs, a better program or programing. I have become weary of church clubs, conventions, campaigns, and committees. I have become nauseated with theological hairsplitting, hallelujah hucksters, hosanna hootenannies, and holy holidays that are neither. I have become disgusted with competitive churches, divisive denominations, separatist sects, and organized organizations. They are all born of the same secular, systemized, spirit that made America a great economic power, but the same mind set and philosophy will never make her a great spiritual power. It is time to break down the scaffolding and expose the real structure of The Faith. I think it is time to get back to the farm faith I saw and experienced on the family farm in the 1950s and 1960s; Christians living in a mutual love and fellowship whether Baptist or Advent.

21

Busybody Bees

RECENTLY, I WAS PREPARING a message for my flock at the Emmanuel Baptist Church in Ellsworth, Maine, when I came across an illustration about honeybees. Whenever I hear the name "honeybee", my mind automatically returns to a pleasant time on the family farm in Perham, Maine, and the three years my dad and I kept honeybees.

Bees are very important to mankind (one of God's great creations) because of their trips back and forth between flowers and fruit trees. They transfer pollen among flowering plants and bushes and between fruit trees of all kinds. This cross-pollination is necessary for the fruits and the foods necessary for sustaining life on this planet. Because of our pastor's interest in the hobby, dad got interested and when dad got interested in something so did I! The first year of this joint-hobby we ordered three colonies of bees through the mail; yes, through the mail! They were a specific classification of bee called 'Italian-Bees', noted for their ability to produce large supplies of honey and their heartiness for surviving in the difficult winter of Maine. It was a summer in the 1960's that my education about bees began, and little did I know the wealth of future illustrations for my sermons. I can still see in my memory those three white bee hive boxes setting beside the old potato house next to my boyhood home. As the warm spring air turned the nearby pastures into a yellow (dandelions) carpet, the activity of the hive increased daily. Pretty soon thousands of bees were returning to the hive carrying yellow pollen on their legs. What a sight to see them busily going about their job of collecting the main ingredient for making 'honey', and in this case 'blackstone honey'!

It wasn't long however, before I learned that not all busy-bees are busy. Dad taught me that a hive usually was made up of three kinds of bees. The 'worker' honeybee was the mainstay of the hive. Besides gathering the pollen, the 'worker' also kept the hive cool on the summer by creating a natural air-conditioner by flapping their wings at the entrance of the hive. They also were busy helping to raise the next generations of bees. The main member of the hive was the queen bee. One per hive was ideal. I remember the third summer of our experimentation with honeybees when we had too many queens for the number of hives we had and the hives were constantly dividing: they call it 'swarming'! Our three hives expanded to well over a dozen hives before that summer was over. This might sound like a good thing to anybody but a beekeeper. The constant swarming so weakened the original hives that they produced little honey and few survived the winter because they were too weak, and the news hives were too small to survive either. If there is only one head the hive will thrive, and then there are the drones!

In every hive there are a number of male bees. There are the non-productive members of the hive except in one area. Much larger than the worker bees, but much smaller than the queen bee, these drones usually spent their time just buzzing around and eating the labor of others: the hive's honey. Once they fertilize the virgin queen-bee their purpose and usefulness is over. They make no comb and no honey and they can't even sting! If they somehow survive the summer, they are killed by the workers before winter when the honey flow slackens! Yet in the bees of a hive I have seen a parallel to people in society.

I have found it interesting that the human society is a lot like the bee fraternity. We have queens and workers and drones. The drones of a society or even a church ought to be thankful they are not bees! *"For we hear that there are some which walk among you disorderly, working not at all, but are busybodies."* (II Thessalonians 3:11)

22

Four Skies

AMONG THE SOUVENIRS I treasure most in the scrapbook of my memory are the pictures of the sky over my family's homestead in the north country of Maine. I was encouraged once again this week to 'look up' by an article in the bulletin of the church I pastor on the coast of Maine, but still two hundred miles from my beloved homestead. The lady who does our weekly service announcements in print had some space at the bottom of page two to fill, so she put in the story of a young man who had found a $20 bill on the sidewalk of the street where he lived. From that time onward, the story says that he never looked up. His eyes were focused on his next big score, so for the rest of his life he had only one view: downward. In a space of 40 years he recorded what he found and the total of his accumulation was: 29,514 buttons, 53,137 pins, 97 pennies, a bent back and a miserable disposition! He failed to see all those beautiful sights and sites that one can only see by looking up. I am thankful that from an early age I learned this admonition from the prophet Isaiah: *"Drop down, ye heavens, from above, and let the skies pour down righteousness."* (Isaiah 45:8) The sky holds some wonderful treasures if you look.

As in any place, there are four kinds of sky you see each day, even on a rural potato/dairy farm in the backwoods of Aroostook County. First, there is the day sky divided between morning and afternoon. On any given day the sky might be a gray color filled with threatening storm clouds that will either deliver a much needed rain or shower, or a blanket of winter snow. Or on any given day it might be blue in color dotted with billowing clouds, or on some days just a clear blue sky. In the spring of the year it is a dull blue reflecting the season just passed, but in the autumn of the year it is a bright blue.

Second, there is the dusk sky that ushers in a night of rest. How I uses to love to set on the front porch of my boyhood home and watch the fire-ball sink into the western horizon. Depending on the day sky, the sky at dusk could either reveal the glorious glow of the sun slowly fading below the hills of Perham, or the rays of the sun reflecting off the low hanging clouds hugging the distant landscape. Each was spectacular to witness.

Third, there was the dark sky. Most people go inside at the advent of night, but I have always been a night person. Some of the greatest sky shows I have ever observed have been at night. For those of you who haven't had the privilege of seeing a northern night sky you will probably never understand my love affair of the heavenly 'northern lights'. They are like huge spotlights streaking up into the dark night, the multi-color arches of an Aurora Borealis is beyond marvelous to behold, it is almost a spiritual experience. Spanning the northern sky with their fiery columns, the night takes on almost divine scenery. Each time I see the splendor of that sight I am reminded that its beacon is pointing me to my real home, and then there are those nights when 'the stars' come out in all their glory. I am reminded when I reread the creation story that *"He made the stars also!"* (Genesis 1:16) as if it were an afterthought, yet the stars have given me some of the best night shows in my life. City dwellers have blocked out the stars with their artificial lights, but on a clear night over the homestead every star in our galaxy is real!

Fourth, there is the dawn sky. I have left the best for last. No doubt there is a beauty in all the skies mentioned, but the dawn sky is the best in my opinion. It is at dawn that you can see Venus and Mercury, the morning stars, the brightest and best of the stars. It is at that time when night merges with morning and no matter how dark the night has been there is a new hope and a new joy in the beginning of a brand new day (Psalms 118:24)!

23

Individual Influence

UNDER THE SHADOW OF a world war a young man sat looking towards his future and fate; he was fighting for the grace to accept the inevitable, the detour in his life that would not only radically change his life but how he would live and where he would live that life?

The Blackstone boy was country born and county bred. All his life he knew there was a bigger world than Perham, but he saw little of it until in 1944 Uncle Sam came-a-calling. From a little hamlet in the northern woods of Maine, he travelled the Atlantic twice to finish that war and to help keep the peace after the bloodiest war this planet have ever seen! But his service for his country had detoured his plans for college and a career in sports medicine. Things had changed dramatically for him. Gradually he came to realize that he would surrender his university ambitions, give up the world beyond Perham, and go back to the family homestead and be a farmer like his father and grandfather and a couple of fathers before. He wrestled with his decision to return, but in the end he packed his army bag, said goodbye to his comrades, quietly went back home, and married his sweetheart.

Steadily and successfully he applied himself to the task of helping his father and uncle care for the land of their forefathers (he would be the fifth generation to farm the homestead). His manner of life became a wonderful example of faithfulness to his neighbors and his ever increasing family. He labored long hours seven days a week, three hundred and sixty-five days a year, but he always had time to be found in his place of worship whenever the doors of his small country church were open! His first love was the mid-week prayer meeting where he led in prayer for the needs of all: family and friends. He eventually taught the men's Sunday school class, a position he held late into his life. The church made him a deacon very early after his return, and as the older men were carried out, often by him, one by one to their final resting place in FairView Cemetery, he became the oldest member of the board of deacons into his 90s, the recognized spiritual, intellectual, moral, and religious leader of the church and his community.

Paul once told the Corinthians Christians, *"Brethren, let every man, wherein he is called, therein abide with God."* (I Corinthians 7:24) If that is true of any man it is true of Wendell E. Blackstone, my father. My dad had many dreams when he was young, some I have just heard about in these last few years of his life, yet he accepted God's choice and became a man of the soil and a man of the Scriptures. His life reminds me of a little poem written about Zebedee, the father of James and John, the apostles of Jesus. It goes:

> "To some Christ calls: leave boat and bay,
> And white-haired Zebedee?
> To some the call is harder: stay,
> And mend the nets for me!"

Dad has never stood before a class of high school and junior high school students as his oldest daughter and younger son have; he has never pastored a church and taken missions trip to Australia and India as I have; he has never healed the sick as his youngest daughter has, and he has never carried on transactions worth millions of dollars as his youngest son has, but as a small-time dairy and potato farmer he has exerted a spiritual influence on so many beyond his family that any man, including this man, would covet.

24

Worthy Walk

HAVE YOU EVER FOUND a setting place to watch people walk by, mall or park? I have been fascinated for years with the strides of the individuals that have strolled before my eyes. By the way people walk you can tell a lot about that person; about what is happening in their lives. If a man passes you in the mall walking with a quick pace, you can be assured that he is trying to find his wife so that he can get out of that place. If a couple passes you in the park by hand in hand walking at a slow pace, you can be assured that they are in love and time has lost its meaning. If a woman passes you by running, you can be assured that she thinks she is overweight and needs to shed a few pounds. Where did I learn about striding you might ask? Where was I taught to watch the steps of people? Where did I first see that our walk is important? The answer to all three questions is from in a man who had a "... *walk worthy of God.*" (I Thessalonians 2:12)

    I cannot remember when my Grandfather Blackstone first took my hand and we went for a walk, but this I have never forgotten: I couldn't keep up! I do remember well that Grandpa Carroll had a tremendous stride, and his steps were always swift. He was a man who knew how to work at only one speed: flat out! From milking to planting to milking again, he moved with a stride unmatched. His steps were powerful, productive, and purposeful. No wasted sidetracks with Grandpa, and when haying season arrived it seemed that Carroll only picked up the pace. He knew clearly the time window he had to get the winter feed into the barn for the Holstein herd was limited, and he used every minute and every individual, including his son's oldest boy, to get the task accomplished as soon as possible; though well into his 60s at the time and me in my teens, I still couldn't keep up with that stride: summer hay time or autumn harvest time.

Grandpa not only had a walking and working stride, but a living and loving stride as well. Grandpa never believed in changing his stride work place or worship place. He never used his stride to wander very far from the straight and narrow (Matthew 7:14), and he never used his exemplary steps to lead another down a garden path, especially his grandson. Grandpa was one of the greatest, if not the greatest man to stroll in and out of my life, and after nearly 40 years of separation I am still trying to keep up with his stride; not an easy task in this difficult day and evil age.

I have come again to the anniversary of my grandfather's passing. Forty years ago upon returning from a fishing trip to northern Quebec, Canada with my father-in-law, Stacy Meister, and my brother-in-law, Larry Fox, I was told of my dear grandfather's death. This anniversary always takes me back to the mid-60s when one morning grandpa didn't stroll out of his house (which I own now) as usual. Grandpa had had his first heart attack and they didn't expect him to survive. I remember standing outside his home and praying that God would allow me to walk with him once more this side of eternity, and I would do my best with the Lord's help to keep up with him. God answered that prayer and gave me almost a decade of walks, but in the summer of 1975, far away from the Blackstone homestead; a second heart attack took one of my inspirations to glory. I must admit the walk to and from the FairView Cemetery was a very difficult journey, for I wondered if I could walk without him. But I found as the days and months and years passed that in our many walks together grandfather had taught me how to walk alone, plod on, stroll forward, and though my stride wasn't and hasn't been comparable to his, I still walk and work and live and love in a stride I first learned at the feet of the master!

25

Fanner Bees

THE ONLY HOBBY MY dad and I enjoyed together in my childhood, besides brook trout fishing, was keeping honey bees. For three summers during my junior high into my high school years, our backyard was alive with the buzzing of Italian honeybees. I learned a lot about spiritual things those few hives of bees, and I will never forget the first time I approached one of our hives and heard the distinct hum of the fanner bees.

It was a warm evening in mid-summer; a mid-summer's night dream? A full moon highlighted a northern Maine sky. The shadows of the three white bee hives could be seen clearly against the dark background of an in-ground potato house that rose directly behind the colony. The side hill on which the three hives stood was bathed in a soft afterglow of a wonderful summer's day as I approached the front of the hives. A slight breeze could be felt on my face and seen in the trees that lined the driveway between me and the side hill. Above the quite noise of a gentle breeze I heard it, another soft sound. It came from the front of one of the hives; a sibilant, persistent, drawing sound. Like the advancing, retreating waves of a somber sea, the sound rolled outward, constant, steady, and captivating. Creeping close to the first hive, I saw a group of bees standing with their heads lowered, and their backs turned towards the center of the narrow entrance into the hive. Their tiny wings were rotating, fluttering so rapidly that I couldn't really see them moving, despite the bright moonlight. It wasn't until the next morning I learned from my dad about the value of the 'fanner bee' to the bee fraternity!

Dad explained to me that the bees I saw in front of the hive the night before were responsible for keeping the bee hive cool and fresh and sweet. Together their collective movement caused by the fanning of their wings drew the bad air through the entrance of the hive, while the pure, clean air was sucked in through other parts of the hive. I marveled again at the mystery of the bee hive, one of God's great creative works. One of His wondrous handiworks making provision through the few for the benefit of the many. Nature's own air-conditioners that bring comfort and health to a community of bees living together in the confined spaces of a bee hive. Think of it; standing all day fanning your wings, working up a sweat yourself, so that others may be comfortable and sweat-free. Wearing yourself out for the good of your community!

I don't know how often I went to the hives on the homestead during the summers of my boyhood to watch the bees and listen to the fanner bees doing their job. Despite the busyness of the hive, worker bee's fling in and out carrying the pollen that created the sweetest honey I have ever tasted, the fanner bees stayed at their post flapping their wings in a steady, cooling manner. On a clam day, when there was no breeze, no wind, you could feel the strong current created by the fanner bees. Those infinitesimal wings rotating in unison, laboring together, making a draft so strong it could be felt by the farmer's son. Just imagine if we could get such cooperation in the Church?

As I sit in thought years later, I have again set my mind on the lesson of the fanner bees: drawing out the bad air and letting in the good air. Isn't that how people who call themselves Christians (Acts 11:46) ought to be known? If we only had enough 'fanners' in our Christian communities, what a fresh and refreshing place the Church would be. It was the Apostle Paul who once wrote, maybe after visiting a bee hive: *"For we are unto God a sweet savor of Christ."* (II Corinthians 2:15) Are we fanning the sweet savor, the faithful flavor of Christ in our homes, our churches, and our communities?

26

Young Giver

I SIT ONCE AGAIN before the computer screen of my laptop with a memory to sermonize. Two events have sparked this remembrance from the 'homestead' file in my brain. The first took place last week when I was catching up on my diary. A note I had put in an old journal concerning a gift my youngest brother gave me in 1981 during a difficult time in my life. The second took place just yesterday at the Emmanuel Baptist Church of Ellsworth, Maine were I am the pastor. Though the events are separated by twelve years, it was their marriage in my mind that helped me understand more clearly Jesus instruction, *"Give, and it shall be given unto you; good measure, pressed down, and shaken together, running over, shall men give into your bosom."* (Luke 6:38)

In my little southern pine lined church, the acoustics in the back of the sanctuary are quite poor. Despite the short distance to the pulpit rarely does a Sunday go by that I don't get a complaint by someone that they couldn't hear some of the things I was saying? Because we have become slaves to hearing devices, ear aids and elderly amplifiers, we don't think we hear when we really do. The problem today isn't with our hearing, but our listening. Ninety and nine percent of the time the problem with hearing could be solved if the dear saint who comes to church early to get the back seat would simply move up to the front where there are always plenty of empty pews. Most never do, creatures of habit, and a quick exit when the service is over! Despite encouragement, most prefer to sit in the back and keep complaining they can't hear. Is it just another excuse for not really wanting to listen? I have come to the conclusion that the same problem exists in the ministry of giving. We might give more if we would listen more.

I have always lived among givers. My homestead in Perham, Maine has produced over the years much grain and many givers. I could fill a book; (actually I am attempting to do just that) if I listed all the sacrificial gifts of my grandparents and parents, aunts and uncles, cousins and brothers and sisters. Through my life I have witnessed some extraordinary acts of giving, and I have learned that givers produce givers! I would like to share this one story of sacrifice to illustrate all the times the members of my family have helped me out; something that continues to this day!

We had just returned from Doctor Hamlin's (an urologist) office with a sobering diagnosis that our 18-month-old daughter, Marnie, would have to undergo a major surgery to correct a birth defect that was slowly destroying her kidneys and bladder. Ever since Marnie was four months old we knew that this day would probably come, but we prayed the Lord would heal her without an operation, but healing would come through an operation. To take some pressure off and to get away from reality, my wife and I decided to go up to the family farm and to participate in the annual autumn potato harvest. As we spent the day with our family, the conversation, however, seemingly always came back to Marnie's upcoming surgery, not digging. Everyone was concerned, but the talk was positive and encouraging and prayerful. My wife and I began to feel a bit better sensing the support and love of family and friends from Perham. Just before we headed back to our pastorate in Westfield my youngest brother Michael handed me an envelope with $100 of his potato harvesting money inside. His only comment was: "I've been listening, and I thought this would help Marnie!" My brother is going to end up as the greatest giver of us all because of God's blessing on his life, but I know where that spirit of giving began. It started when as a young man he learned how to listen to the needs of others!

27

Farming Farmer

A NUMBER OF YEARS ago my wife Coleen cross-stitched a wall hanging for my father, Wendell. On that piece of handiwork was this little poem: "This land my own, and by my labors here, I have made myself a farm. Found peace no man can harm a life I understand. This land my own, and by my labor's here, I have made myself a man." When I think of dad, 'farmer' is the first word that comes to my mind and memory. In the rural community where I grew up, there were many who farmed, but few farmers. In the same farming community today, there are few farming (actual there are no farmers left in Perham; all the land that is tilled is farmed by people living outside of Perham) and this Blackstone farmer has had to give up the plow after over 40 years of sowing seed (Dad is in his 90s). *"And Jesus said unto him, No man, having put his hand to the plough, and looking back, is fit for the kingdom of God."* (Luke 9:62) Once Dad set his course as a farmer, he never looked back, he never looked around, and he never looked away!

I remember the last time I asked my father this question: "How's the farm?" His reply was the same I had heard all my life: "Still hard plowing!" Dad's job after the annual fall harvest was to plow the land reaped in preparation for another spring planting. One of my favorite labors on the homestead was plowing. It was my father that taught me the joy of cutting the soil. If you have never plowed a rock-infested, ledge-bottom field you probably don't know of what I speak. It is a thrilling experience to plow a few stony fields with a sharp plow and a reliable John Deere (a tractor we plowed with). I remember well the first time my father took me to the top of the hill, out behind Grandpa's place (a place I own today), and instructed me in the finer points of fall plowing. I still recall the stories Dad told of the days he use to plow with horses and a one bottom plow. Dad was clear about keeping the plowshare in the furrow, and guiding's one's course by a tall spruce tree at the end of the field. Dad used the same principle to plant the potatoes in the spring. There has never been a farmer (in my opinion) that could plant a straighter row or plow a straighter furrow than Wendell E. Blackstone. Kind of like his life, straight and true to its course. I remembered him speaking of those that forced the plow; the plow must be pulled not pushed. Dad's favorite author, Vance Havner, would say, he would say: *"A lot of energy can be spent trying to push what can only be pulled!"* Dad would say that it was his responsibility to guide, and it was the tractor's responsibility to pull. He taught me to keep my eye on the goal, not the ground. If I was to plow a straight furrow I must resist the temptation to be distracted by the plow or the Farmall (another tractor we used to plow with). I have found that the Christ-like life is to be lived in the same manner; in the philosophy of the plowman.

    I recall my farming father as a man who gave everything to the farm. If he wasn't up by four or five he thought he was late for work. Being his own boss I never could figure out at first why? I too at times was shaken awake with, "Wake up, we're late!" on the morning I would help him milk before we were off to do some kind of field work. It was 3:45 AM, but we were late? I don't know it then, but I realize it now, Dad had an employer, the farm. It might be thirty-below zero, yet the farm work still needed doing! It might be mid-winter, or mid-summer, no matter, the farm came first. Why, because dad was a farmer, not a lawyer or a doctor, and it takes a 'farmer' to farm a farm! I have come to the conclusion the same precept applies to Christianity; it takes Christ and a Christian to spell Christianity. It takes a committed, dedicated believer to be one too!

28

Admirable Afterglow

TODAY, I WAS REMEMBERING a story I once used in a devotional I had written for the flock (Washington Street Baptist Church) I was shepherding in Eastport, Maine a few years ago. It seems a mother and her small daughter were walking one day passed the home in Springfield, Illinois where Abraham Lincoln had once lived; a place that had become a memorial and museum to the famous president. The lights were still on inside the house giving the home a warm and inviting appeal to the little girl. The two paused for a few moments in front of the residence, which had been opened to the public. As the mother told her daughter about President Lincoln and the great lose the nation felt after his tragic death, the little lass seemed to be taking in every word as her mother finished the mini-history lesson. Then as they were about ready to leave the little girl spoke up and said, "Look Mommy. When Mr. Lincoln went away he left the lights on!" Though my grandfather Blackstone left the homestead many years ago (1975) for a better homestead in heaven, he left an afterglow as Paul encouraged us all to do: "*To make ourselves an ensample unto you to follow us.*" (II Thessalonians 3:9)

Each time I return to the family homestead in Perham, Maine, as I did recently, I have to pass the bleak, black gravestone of Carroll F. Blackstone. Despite the cold, dark granite, a warmth still radiates from the farm he once tilled and toiled on, and the house he once lived in and loved; my home now! Though he departed decades ago, he left the lights of Christian love, peace, and joy still burning in my life and the life of my family and we still bask in the afterglow to this day. I still see by his lasting testimony how I ought to walk in this very dark and depressing world. That is why I write so often of grandfather and his homestead. His is a fitting Blackstone biography to get direction and discernment from. Often when I am traveling through a rough and rugged period in my life, I am lead through that black lane, gloomy land by the shining 'ensample' Grandpa left for me to follow, and I believe he would have me follow him the same way Paul challenged his fellow-believers to follow him: *"Be ye followers of me, even as I also am of Christ."* (I Corinthians 11:1) Not only does Grandpa Carroll's afterglow still light up my life, his influence is still felt on the farm and those still attached to the homestead. Carroll's branch is still bearing fruit today. He lived such a life that he left behind a wonderful spiritual legacy that has been a positive, Christian influence on a generation of young people he never knew. Grandpa has long since departed, yet his memory is still remembered by so many. Grandpa has long since passed on, yet his money is still providing for needs in his family. Grandpa has long since gone, yet his monument is still a beacon to guide us back to the homestead he loved, and especially the little white church on the corner. Part of immortality, I believe, is not only in eternity, but living on in the lives of people we have fathered, have furthered, and have financed us. Each time I enter the barn-shaped house on the side hill I remember the light that once lived there. Its glow reached beyond the potato and pasture lands that surround that home into the very heart of Perham. Grandpa's glow overshadowed more than his family, but countless friends as well. The impact of his light, though dimmed by death, has yet to be extinguished, and if I have anything to say or do about it, I will continue to fuel the lamp, brighten the torch, fan the flame, so that the generations to come will know why the farm in the north Maine woods still has such an admirable afterglow! Jesus taught that in this world we are to be a light (Matthew 5:13) and after this world a glow (John 15:16)!

29

Good Gardener

THE AIR IS ZERO outside, and a foot of snow covers the ground, yet, inside my study at the Emmanuel Baptist Church in Ellsworth, Maine it feels like spring. Why such a transformation, a contrast? It is simple: my mind and memory are once again focused on my boyhood farm, my childhood homestead and a springtime gardener.

My grandfather Blackstone was not only a farmer, but the gardener of the family when I was just a little lad, and sometimes I was called on to be his assistant. Grandpa loved to see things grow, but he also loved to see those things grow neatly. To keep the lawns around the homestead buildings beautiful and blooming grandpa often asked me to help, but Grandpa was always the moving and motivating spirit in the midst of lavish lawns, towering trees, fragrant flowers, and ornate orchards. Though there was plenty of family on the 720 acre farm, Grandpa was the one who saw that the vegetable garden was tended correctly. Grandpa was one of those rare individuals who truly had a 'green' thumb! Every seed for the vegetable garden was tenderly fondled when it arrived from the Vessie's Seed Company in Prince Edwards Island, Canada each spring. Every bush around Grandpa's home was pruned regularly, as were the apple trees in the orchard behind his house. Whether shrub, bush, flowering plant, or tree, each responded to the touch of Grandpa's gentle and gracious hand and grew accordingly, and so did I!

Grandpa the gardener, like me, was quiet, unobtrusive person by his very nature; perhaps that is why we got along so well;

kindred-spirits. He didn't mind being alone; a man at peace with himself, others, and the world around him. He was also at peace with God and his garden. Perhaps that is why his garden produced for him as it did. From barrels of turnips to bushels of cucumbers to baskets of beans to buckets of corn, Grandpa's garden always yielded enough to feed the families on the homestead and many of his Perham friends as well. As I would often pass the garden located just below his house on my way to do something for father on the farm, I would see him working away along the rows. It was a picture of serenity, stillness, and solitude that still resides in the back on my memory, and when I think of it on cold winter days like today, the image of Grandpa and his garden makes my soul and fills my spirit with a profound peace. As the Holstein herd grazed on the hillside beyond his house, Grandpa gleaned the increase of his spring and summer labor of love, and he seemed to manage those marvelous miracles year after year in the face of insect raids, oppressive heat, and insufficient rain.

As I matured from boyhood to manhood, I was drawn closer to Grandpa's company. I enjoyed the quiet retreats into the orchard when Grandpa would ask me to prune the apple trees in fall. I treasured now the times I could peacefully ponder the purpose of life as I mowed his lawn (I was the first person he entrusted his lawn too-I only realized the honor later in life), or weeded his garden. Grandpa perceived my quiet side and my need to be alone and eventually I learned a day alone in nature with God as your only companion are the best days of all. Often he would silently slip up behind me, or fall in step beside me, but without fail would only smile sweetly or speak softly! Never once do I recall hearing him lift up his voice in anger; strife and swearing were not in his DNA, and he never disrupted my daydreaming, for I perccive now he knew there was more growing in his garden than just beets and beans; for he was cultivating and caring for a boy, a Barry along with those other vegetables. Carroll Blackstone was not only my Grandpa; he was also my gardener: *"Apollos watered; but God gave the increase."* (I Corinthians 3:6)

30

Wonderful Wonder

IN THE ADVANCEMENTS OF mankind, we have lost something irreplaceable: the wonder of God and His world. With the urbanization of the city swallowing up the utopia of the country, we have lost the simple awe and quiet inspiration that comes from walking along a brook, working in a barnyard, and whistling with a bird. With our over dependence on technology, we have lost the excitement that comes from living with God and God alone. Today, most people are surrounded with traffic not trees, streets not streams, sidewalks not side hills. Their only stimulation comes from the manipulative media who glorifies the glitter and glamour of urban life verses country life. Malls have replaced meadows, neon lights have replaced night lights, and the telescope has been replaced by the television. Unless it is video or VCR, digital or DHS, people rarely wonder at the sights or sites they are seeing. The Psalmist wrote a marvellous exhortation we still need to heed and hear today: *"Remember his marvellous works that He hath done; his wonders . . . "* (Psalm 105:5) George Beverly Shea, Billy Graham's soloist, taught us to sing this song: "There's the wonder of sunset at evening, the wonder at sunrise I see; but the wonder of wonders that thrills my soul is the wonder that God loves me. There's the wonder of springtime and harvest, the sky, the stars, the sun; but the wonder of wonders that thrill my soul is the wonder that's only begun." When was the last time you wondered about anything other than the stock market rising or falling, a football, baseball, or basketball play, or how they made a particular movie scene so real?

Homestead Homilies

I am thankful for the wonder of a country boyhood. On my family farm in Perham, Maine in the 1950s and 1960s I had a real childhood. Today before most boys are teenagers they have become old and aged, critical and cynical, wasted and used up. They have been robbed of 'The Wonder Years' by the sensual, sinful, and sordid society they live in. As for me, I lived in the sweet solitude of a rural ranch isolated by distance and dignity. No perverts were preying on our innocence, just wonderful examples of manhood and womanhood, whether family or friend, teacher or preacher. No pimps were plundering the purity of youth, just helpful bus drivers and janitors, coaches and church leaders. No wonder I wish my children could have grown up slowly, as I did, for I fear they lost the wonderment of children, the wonder of youth; despite my attempt to keep them young as long as possible; to keep them innocent despite their years.

I am thankful for the wonder of a backyard and a barnyard. For most a backyard is only a few feet of lawn between their home and their neighbor's house. So it is with me now, but 'once upon a time' (I know to most this sound like a fairy tale!) I had a backyard in my barnyard; acres of pasture land and woodland to roam and to call home. My lot wasn't to escape into the 'tube', but into the trees. My world wasn't a fantasy or fascination with mechanical gadgets and technological games, but of forest and fields. For most kids today the backyard is the back room and a Nintendo, or a Wee! Hemmed in by walls, their minds can't develop properly the ability to wonder, to know the difference between fantasy and reality-is that why we have kids killing kids? Granted, the modern kid can handle the control mechanism of a video game with exceptional speed and dexterity, but they soon get lost in the real world as we are sadly realizing. I learned nothing of Mario in my boyhood, backyard, barnyard, but I did discover the mysteries and the majesty of lakes and larks, sparrows and swallows, bees and brooks. I simply ask: which uplifts the soul more? Who is really in touch with life and living?

31

Archer's Arrows

YESTERDAY I WAS THE guest speaker at the chapel service of Temple Christian Academy in Ellsworth, Maine, where my children go to school. My text was "As arrows are in the hand of a mighty man; so are children of the youth." (Psalm 127:4) With the psalmist, I drew some similarities between archery and adolescence. During my message, I also used illustrations from my boyhood when I use to play Cowboys and Indians with my cousins.

My early archery equipment was all homemade and handmade. If it was my turn, and in those days we did take turns, to play the part of an Indian attacking my cowboy cousins, I would first have to make my bow and then some arrows. A young poplar branch about three feet long would be sufficient for the bow, and a length of bailer twine would be adequate for the bow string. Tied tightly at both ends I would make it as firm as I possibly could, but loose enough not to harm my prey; I wasn't out to kill my cowboy cousin, how things have changed in the game's kids play today! The arrows were also manufactured very rapidly. A few shorter and thinner lengths off the old poplar tree were quickly whittled into shape. A notch in one end and a sharp-dull point at the other end usually finished the process for creating my bow and arrow set. I wouldn't attach any feathers because that was too time consuming, besides the chickens were never cooperative with me, egg gathering or feather gathering. Once I got as many twigs as I wanted for arrows, I would usually put them in a discarded feed bag which would act as my quiver. Flung over my shoulder, I was ready to make war on my cousins, the cowboys; who by this time had made their pretend rifles and pistols out of old wood, with the odd cap gun mixed in.

These Blackstone homestead wars would often take place in one of two cow barns, or in the barnyard somewhere. Sometimes, the struggle between paleface and Redman would spill over into the forest lands that surrounded our boyhood home. If we fought the battle in the barn, a fort made out of hay or straw bales was usually constructed first. Creeping up on Fort Haymow wasn't easy, but it was necessary because the range of my bow and arrow was quite limited. Often I would get shot before I got within range or got my first arrow off, but sometimes the sentry on duty would miss my approach. Pulling my straightest arrow from my quiver, I would load the crooked stick into the twine. Realizing very early that a warped arrow flies crooked; I had to compensate for its erratic flight. If my calculations were right I would often bring down a cousin, but if I missed I would receive back such a volley of cap gun noise you would think you were in a real fire fight. Often the mini-war would last only a few minutes with all participants lying dead across the walls of our imaginary fort. It was then we would awaken and I would trade my genuine Blackstone homestead archery set for a genuine homemade homestead Winchester rifle that my Cousin Dale had made that very morning before the big battle. The fort would be repaired and before you knew it I was the lookout at Fort Haymow!

If children are like arrows, then they have to be straightened out before they can fly right. David said that we were all "sharpened in iniquity" (Psalms 51:5) and in "sin. . . . conceived", so the importance of our upbringing is vital. There is a war raging in this world and children seem to be the fodder. Unlike my cousins and I, we would rise after each battle; too few children get a second chance today. The call of Christ needs to be proclaimed afar: *"Suffer the little children to come unto me, and forbid them not: for such is the kingdom of God."* (Mark 10:14) Shot right, they too will hit the goal!

32

Land Lamentation

IT IS THE MIDDLE of winter and a cold wave has frozen my body, but not my brain. It is still able to turn time backward and make me a boy again; back on the family farm in northern Maine I called home in my childhood. While we are in the melancholy days of winter here, better known by us Maineaic as 'cabin fever days', it is springtime in my soul each time I turn the clock back, but lately something else has invaded my memory. I have started to compare what I remember then to what I know now, and like the Hebrew prophet Jeremiah, *"I am a man that hath seen affliction."* (Lamentations 3:1)

I am mourning again, for a prophecy of the 1960s is being fulfilled in the 1990s. I was raised on 60's music. One song I remember well was sung by Joni Mitchell. In that revolutionary hit, she sung about man plundering and pillaging this planet for his own personal profit. One phrase that is haunting me today is, *"They stole paradise, and put in a parking lot!"* Recently in a visit back home to the homestead, I took a good look at what was happening to my old country county; as farm after farm shuts down, mall after mall starts up. Land that once was covered with livestock and lilacs is now covered with pavement and parking lots. Asphalt, not alfalfa is now the cover crop of choice in Aroostook County. Land that once gave us broccoli now gives us boutiques. Land that once grew spuds is now growing stores. As the prophets of old lamented over the destruction of invading armies, I lament over the near sighted contractors who think they have made the land more valuable by covering it up. We have traded a paradise for a parking lot. The velvet soil that once covered my beloved county is now shrouded in Velcro! We have made a poor trade, I think!

Recently I was reading W. Phillip Keller's wonderful book, *God is My Delight*, and in it he made these comments that I think apply to my boyhood home: *"As a race we claim the name homo sapiens, the wise ones, when in truth we are the opposite. No other creature on the planet has so devastated its resources or squandered its treasures with utter abandon. We claim to be so superior to lesser life forms when in reality we are so stupid. A gracious God has placed us in a gorgeous garden of His design. We in turn prefer to turn around and trash it; until it becomes a desert."* I fear this for my county, my homestead, for the men and women who love the land are being forced out by outsiders who have no love for the integrity of the soil. They see it only for the profit they can make, and when they make it, they will leave it to destroy another lovely field of clover somewhere else. They will abandon their asphalt field to find another homestead, another dairy farm and turn it into a strip mall, or a department store!

My heart is heavy today because my homestead seems to be on the hit list of bottom line bureaucrats who want to turn my childhood paradise into another parking lot of abandoned farm equipment. I regret that my wealth is not in the bank, but in my accounts in heaven, for if it were, I would turn all their parking lots back into a paradise of fields and forests again, and then I think of my theology and I smile. If you believe like I do, there is a day coming, and very soon at that, when the King of Kings and the Lord of Lords will return to this planet and will restore this earth to its Eden glory. No longer will we wander in malls but in meadows, no longer walk along boulevards but by brooks!

Today the earth groans (Romans 8:22) and the land laments, but soon and very soon it will rejoice and laugh again in the marvellous newness of recreation. I can't wait to see my county again transformed and reformed into the purpose God created it for!

33

Dale Dew

TODAY, AS I SAT in my study, I thought again of my homestead. The reason for this remembrance was the subject matter I was studying at the time. I was putting together a devotional on the topic of dew. Instantaneously, my memory recalled the days on the family farm in northern Maine when the most important thing that happened was the dropping of the dawn dew on the forest and fields of the farm: *"The heavens shall give their dew!"* (Zechariah 8:12)

Being the firstborn son of a potato/dairy farmer and having been raised on a fully functioning homestead, I know something about dew. I remember my Dad speaking of the blessing of the dew. In a dry Maine summer, the dew was sometimes the only moister the potato plants and the oat stalks would get for weeks on end. The late summer dew supplemented the absence of the latter rains. A heavy morning dew would often fool you into thinking that it had rained the night before. Walking through the pasture while herding the Holsteins to the milking shed would result in your overalls getting a soaking, like jumping into the creek. Rogueing in the early morning through waist high potato rows was just like wading through Beaver Brook by the time you got to the end of the field. I have at times had to stop mowing my grandfather's lawn because the dew was so heavy and the wet grass was clogging the mower. Have you ever picked an apple right off the tree still dripping with dew? I have, many times, and there is nothing more delicious and desirable to eat!

Dew is a silent shower without the thunder and the lighting to announce it. It quietly forms in the darkness of the night to water the earth in the brightness of the day. Unseen and unheard, it cools the air and it covers the land refreshing and reviving each and every homestead and homesteader. Father often spoke of how the dew not only watered, but fertilized the fields. As a mid-summer drought took hold, and the potato plants languished under the intense heat, there wilted appearance was sad to observe and fear set in, could they survive? We might go to bed thinking they could not last another day under the scorching sun, and then almost miraculously by the next morning they were growing and glowing again because the dew had fallen. The dew had come again to save the crop and the custodian of the farm. The fruitfulness of the farm could be at least in part contributed to the reclusive rain called dew!

More often than nought, the dew of the earth is created on a clear, calm night. Clouds don't always mean rain, and for the reason I often heard my dad simply ask for heavy dew, rather than a heavy rain. Late in the growing season in Aroostook County, a stiff wind and drenching rain were often more damaging and dangerous to the oats and potatoes than a dew. The gentle mist of the dew was just what the tender plants needed to set the fruit to ripening. The parched ground would respond by drinking in every last drop when the soil was saturated with dew. This invisible irrigation was probably responsible for more bumper crops than any other factor, yet it hasn't gotten the recognition it justly deserves. We often forget our theology when it comes to dew, for I believe long before the Lord gave the world rain (in the disaster and the destruction of Noah's flood), He first used the dew to water His new world: *"And every plant of the field before it was in the earth, and every herb of the field before it grew: for the Lord had not caused it to rain upon the earth, and there was not a man to the till the ground. But there went up a mist (a dew?) from the earth, and watered the whole face of the ground."* (Genesis 2:5–6)

34

Town Tragedy

"Now I lay me down to sleep, I pray the Lord my soul to keep. If I should die before I wake, I pray the Lord my soul to take!" That was my boyhood prayer for most of my early years just before I went off to sleep on my childhood homestead in rural northern Maine. This was the simple petition my parents taught me to teach me the importance of prayer. I remember clearly to this day, though over fifty years have passed, the day I came face to face with *a time to die* (Ecclesiastes 3:2) and that childish supplication!

I was taught that I must come to God in respect and reverence before I could pray even the simplest petition. To approach God properly in prayer first meant I had to quiet down and calm down. I was not coming into the presence of a grandparent or the pastor, but God Himself. I was taught not to play around in prayer. There was a time to kid and fool around with my sister Sylvia, but prayer time, before bedtime, wasn't the time! Even though my supplications were short and simple, I was instructed to pray each with a sincere heart and mind. Stereotype and superficial supplications were not pleasing to God or parent! I am thankful for a father and a mother that taught me from an early age by exhortation and example that I could, even as a small lad, direct my simplest desire and declare my despair to the heavenly Father, and that He heard even a child's prayer and would according to His will answer a child's petition.

The first time these instruction hit home to my heart happened during a town tragedy in our small hamlet of Perham, Maine. The news that my best friend at the time, Randy Tarr, had just lost his youngest brother in a snow sliding accident had struck the residents of Perham hard. Living in a small farming community of a few hundred folks, tragic accidents were rare, this being the only one I remember from my childhood. The whole town was stocked by the terrible news that two young children (both under ten years of age) had died when the slide on which they were riding had slide out into the road by the Perham Elementary School directly into the path of an oncoming car. There was no way the driver could stop, and there was no way the two small boys could live! As Mother sat Sylvia and I down around our kitchen table and told us the sad news, she ended by saying lets pray for the Tarr and Paradis families. My first major crisis and what to pray? I still know what I prayed that day, "Now I lay me down to sleep . . . " It was then I realized the importance of that prayer: 'I pray the Lord my soul to take!" My two fellow school mates at Perham Elementary had gone, quickly, suddenly! My nightly prays had given me confidence to pray in a tragedy, and though I still had to deal with the emotion of facing Randy and his older brother Terry when we meet the next time at school, after that prayer around the kitchen table a great peace and repose settled on me and in my heart making the terrible event tolerable. I learned that prayer was not a penance, but a wonderful promoter of personal peace in a time of tragedy and death.

The day death came to rural Perham; the reality of the importance of prayer came to my soul. Before that day it had been mostly a rite and ritual, a way to please mother and father, but after the Tarr/Paradis tragedy I never questioned the value of prayer again. I will not say I am, or I have become a great man of prayer, but ever since that prayer on the homestead I have practiced and preached of its benefits and blessings, certain benefits and wonderful blessings that can only come through prayers, supplications, and intercessions (I Timothy 2:1–2); any prayer, the Lord's Prayer, yes, even "Now I lay me down to sleep' kind of prayer!

35

Homestead Hedge

I WAS READING MY father's favorite author Vance Havner today, and he brought back a memory from my cherished childhood that I felt I needed to share on paper. The remembered event was when my father and I worked side by side creating two hedges that are still standing today on the property once owned by my folks. The saying by Havner that sparked this recall was, *"God had more in mind than mere geography when he mixed the peaks and the plains!"*

My dad and I have very little in common now-a-days. He still lives in the county of our birth, and I live in a coastal city. He is retired and ninety-two, and I am just reaching, I believe, the zenith of my career as a pastor at 65. He's address is in a VA home, and mine is a simple street address. Nevertheless, we still have one thing in common, and that is a love for the out-of-doors verses the indoors. We both love hills and hallows and hedges. Where some men love the city for its boulevards and bowling alleys and burger joints, dad and I love brooks and birch trees and being alone. I learned to love spruce trees and solitude and streams from my farming, forest-loving father. This is why I fight every day against those who would bring the madhouse of the modern masses into my memory. I live daily in the rat race man calls progress, but I yearn for a hedge to hide behind. A huge, high, homestead hedge, like the one Satan complained about that was surrounding Job: *"Hast not Thou made a hedge about him?"* (Job 1:10) Let me tell you about the hedges of the homestead of my boyhood.

Dad didn't tell me why we were replanting furs from the forest along a fence line behind the old underground potato house that occupied a small knoll behind our home on the High Meadow Road in Perham, Maine, but I still helped him! Just as he didn't tell me why we were relocating trees from the pasture to the east side of our farm house, but I still helped dig the holes. The tiny trees weren't impressive at first, just a few feet tall for the tallest, but as the years passed and the trees grew taller and began to fill in the gap between them, I began to understand why dad and I built those hedges. Because the old farmhouse sets between two open fields, one a meadow and one a pasture, the hedges would act as a natural barrier cutting the strong cross-winds that periodically sweep across the barnyard around our home. In the winter, they were especially important resisting the drifting of the snow into the circler driveway that surrounds the three-story house. In the heat of summer, the hedges acted like giant air filters cooling the hot winds blowing across the barnyard. These were the practical reasons we built the two hedges, but then as the years passed and I left the hedges of my youth I found another important reason why dad and I built those hedges in my childhood.

Hedges are great places to go to get away from it all. Walk behind a hedge and whatever you left behind, stays behind. A hedge shields you from a world gone made, and for a moment, the hedge transports you to another place and maybe, time. In times of tumult, I use to get behind the hedge and just bask in the peace and quiet of its shade. I was a boy when the first tree was planted in the hedge, but by the time I left home the hedge stood tall and proud above me. How often in the madding pace of Ellsworth, the crowded calendar of committee meetings, and the telephone calls that steal away my solitude, that my homestead hedge was just across Park Street. Today, those two hedges dwarf the building they stand beside, where planted to guard. They are a bit worn and a few trees have died, but for me they stand as symbols of stability and solitude!

36

Sparrow Sounds

I HAVE ASKED MYSELF all winter, "Where have all the birds gone?" An avid bird watcher and feeder, I have bemoaned the lack of Black-capped Chickadees at my feeders throughout the winter months here on the coast of Maine where I live. I had even erected a new barn shape feeder in the fall, doubling my feeding capacity, yet fewer and fewer birds came by for a visit, or a feed, until there were none for most of the months of January and February! I feel man in all his progress and advancement is slowly, ever so slowly, polluting the air, the water, and the land making them uninhabitable for the smallest creatures on this planet, namely the songbirds which I love. I can now only dream of the days on the homestead when the birds were plentiful, and there wasn't such a thing as "a" lone sparrow.

A week before spring arrived in Downeast Maine, I finally saw a lone finch flicking seeds out of my giant sunflower seed feeder. With my hopes renewed, I began listening for the return of my favorite spring sound, and yesterday, I was rewarded when I awoke from my slumbering sleep to the melodic music of singing sparrows. I am no expert on sparrows, but I have studied enough to know a sparrow from a sparrow, or at least most of the time. Four of this species of songbirds have become favorites. First, I love the music of the White-throated Sparrow, or Zonotrichia Albicollis. Vance Havner, a bird watching preacher from North Carolina, once described its *"song that begins like the Wedding March lifted octaves beyond human reach."* As the days lengthen, the Whitethroat will sing a mournful 'peabody, peabody, peabody,

peabody' that will be easily recognized in the warming air along the shoreline of Maine. Second, the Chipping Sparrow, or Spizella Passerina, was the artful nest-builder that lined its home with the hairs from off my Dad's Holsteins and occupied the highest rafters in our cow barn. Its high, yet sweet 'tseep, tseep, tseep, tseep' will soon be blending with the spring sounds that makes spring-time one of the most musical seasons of the year. Third, and perhaps, the best known of the singing sparrows, the Melospiza Melodia, or Singing Sparrow will added its 'chimp, chimp, chimp, chimp' to the quartet of sounds coming through my bedroom window, just like they did in the days of my youth. Lastly, there is the House Sparrow, or Passer Domesticus, a constant visitor to the homestead when I was a lad. As with the Chickadee on the coldest day in the winter, this sparrow will sing on the hottest day of the summer its 'chirp, cheep, chirp, cheep, chirp, cheep, chirp cheep' to the silence of the other birds.

 The ancient psalmist speaks of " . . . *a sparrow alone upon the housetop . . .* " (Psalm 102:7) Will this be the sparrow's sad fate one day? Could this be the end awaiting the stirring songs of the sparrows? Birds that love to sing in unison, in chorus, are destined to be soloists? Birds who love to harmonize in great chorales only singing in duets and trios? I can't imagine living the springs and summers of my future with only a few sparrows singing solo! It was in their multitudes and music that I first was drawn to their concerts on the Blackstone homestead. It was in their constant singing that added life to the barnyard of my boyhood. Their melody woke me in the morning of my youth, and their chorus caused me to fall asleep at night in my childhood. "A sparrow sound", God forbid! I live in a city now and I have discovered that few birds like the city, except perhaps the crows. The songbirds left my street years ago to the point I no longer put up my feeders, for what good is a bird feeder without birds?

37

Lesser Light

I HAVE JUST RETURNED from my annual spring fishing trip to the Miramichi River in Upper Blackville, New Brunswick, Canada. It was a great trip with many Black Salmon fishing tales to tell, but on this my first night back to my computer in Ellsworth, Maine, it is not 'a fish story' I wish to record, but an encounter with a full moon, and the memories that heavenly body brought to my homestead mind.

The full moon of which I write was the full moon for the month of April. It shone brightest on the 24th of that month. I drove to my father-in-law's, Stacy Meister, house in its glare through a foggy Northern Maine Sunday night. When I saw it again the next night, I was setting on the porch of Vicker's Camp on the banks of the mighty Miramichi River after a successful day of fishing. Both encounters with this "... *lesser light that rules the night* . . . " (Genesis 1:16), sparked remembrances from my childhood, when that full moon would rise every month over my boyhood home in Perham, Maine.

I recall the evenings that same moon would shine down on a winter wonderland of white. Peeking out from behind a cloud bank, its rays would turn the whole countryside around my boyhood home into a ghostly gray. As the clouds parted and the moonshine was unobstructed, the light reflected off the drifted snow and snow banks turning the landscape heavenly. I can still see in my mind's eye as I looked out my second-story bedroom window at the celestial scene before me. Despite the bitter cold outside and the chill inside (no heat upstairs in the old house), I felt warmer in the glow of that brilliant moon created by my Maker!

    I remember the evenings that same moon would shine down on a summer evening on the front porch of our home. Rover, my childhood dog, would be relaxing in his favorite corner after a busy day guarding the barnyard from passing cars and stray cats as the moon made its way up from behind the eastern hills toward Caribou. Dad would come out from the kitchen for a moment of fresh air before heading off to bed (had to get up early to milk the cows) as the moon shone through the hardwood ridge that overshadowed our old farmhouse. Sylvia, my sister, would be reading as the moon crested the tops of the trees. Mum would come out and say it was time for bed just as the full moon took command of the night sky as the sun died in the western sky toward Perham. I am sixty-five years old and how many full moons I have seen I know not, but last week I stood and shared again as if it were the first time, just as I did the first night I watched one of God's greatest creations take a curtain call over my homestead home.

    I continue to reminisce about the evenings that same moon would shine down in a full harvest moon. Fall is my second most favorite (spring being first) season, and a full harvest moon is one of its highlights. Usually, that special moon came out sometime during the annual potato harvest. It always brought with it a risk of frost, but its brilliance was worth the risk. Besides, we couldn't do much about it anyway! I remember finishing bring in the last potato barrel of the day as the big, white ball rose slowly in the dark autumn sky. As we drove the truck into the potato house, the moon seemed to say, "Good job. Rest awhile. I will guard your field till you return tomorrow!"

    And then there were the full moons that came out in the Spring. In winter the moon is cold, but with the arrival of the spring moon the air is warmer, even at night. The moon allowed you to stay our later, and the afterglow of the moon only reminded you that winter was over and a renewal was around the corner, just like when the moon is full!

38

Morning Moonset

THE MOON HAS BEEN a highlight and has underlined a major truth in my life these last few weeks. After experiencing a full Spring moon on the banks of the Miramichi River in New Brunswick, Canada last month, I watched just a few days ago the only Annular Eclipse I will ever witness in the skies over Ellsworth, Maine. Not since 1875, in the Northeast, has the moon passed between the earth and the sun as it did on Tuesday. The full-moon surrounded by a blazing ring at mid-afternoon was a site and a sight to behold. The Psalmist perhaps spoke of it best when he wrote, "... *abundance of peace so long as the moon endureth.*" (Psalm 72:7) I had one of those days in my youth!

It was one of those clear, chilly nights in spring. A full moon aglow in milky white rose steadily into a star-studded spring sky. A typical country day on the homestead was coming to a close. The barnyard was settling down to a much needed rest and sleep. Hour by hour the moon rose higher and higher from the eastern horizon. Soon every hill and hollow, field and forest on the farm was shining with a bright mantle of light. A lonely moo could be heard from the pasture behind father's huge cow barn. A dark ghostly figure could be seen crossing the road as my dog Rover made his way home from an afternoon excursion to somewhere; the only way of knowing where could be found in the shadow of his smile. The finally cock-a-doodle-doos could be heard from the chicken coup, as the round ball of white escaped the tree line along the ridge. The evening breeze subsided as I got into bed, but I knew I would be up before the moon sat because this was potato planting season on the Blackstone homestead!

W. Phillip Keller once wrote, *"The whole world waits for morning, but before dawn can come, the moon must set!"* I hear Dad up first as I sleepily get out of bed. My job was to get the barn chores done before I headed for the potato house to cut seed. As I made my way out through the pantry, I noticed the moon through the window slowly, steadily, and surely sinking behind the low hills to the west of Perham. The white light of night has turned into a golden glow reflecting the morning sun coming up to the east over Caribou. Stepping into the barnyard, the setting moon spreads it's finally glow over the landscape. Rover barks for joy at its fading splendor as we make our way across the narrow gap between house and barn. Just before I walk through the broad doors in the front of the cow barn, I took one last glimpse and glance at the morning moonset. It's final few minutes and moments of glory capture my attention and imagination and inspiration as you can tell from this homily. Only those who have witnessed the ending of the dark and the beginning of the dawn know the breathless beauty and wondrous wonder of a moonset and as Keller put it: *"the mystery and the majesty of the moment."*

How can such a moment last these many years? How can that final minute still be in my brain? How has that moonset survived all this time? Buried deep in my homestead memory that moonset has survived while countless other events of my childhood have been lost in time. Recently I was embarrassed to admit to my wife I had forgotten the events surrounding our engagement. I couldn't remember the way I proposed, or even how I proposed, now that is bad! Yet a memorable moonset is still locked away, why? Could the answer simply be in the simplicity of the occasion? Majestic in its moments, the moon is only as brilliant as the sun that reflects its brilliance off its face. A morning moonset is only as good and glorious and grand as a spring sunrise! Such is the lesson of the Christian and Christ; only as He reflects His light off our lives. (Matthew 5:14)

39

Homestead Health

IN MY TRAVELS AS a rural pastor, I often have to go to the local hospitals to visit a sick and sometimes dying parishioner, as I did today. Driving the winding, coastal road to the Bar Harbor Hospital this morning, I noticed that spring had finally arrived after a typical long Maine winter. The trees and lawns were starting to get their light green coating, and the highway was crowded with Memorial Day, weekend, first vacation of the year visitors from who know where? Two sure signs that spells *'spring'* on the downeast coast of Maine! Though not in the spring of my life, this morning I felt like I was. As I drove through Hull's Cove visibility was like the old song says, *"On a clear day you can see forever!"* As I made my way into the hospital, a gust of fresh, warm, spring air filled my lungs and it tasted so sweet and pleasant that I hated to exhale. Recently, I have been fighting a few aches and pains that often come with middle age, but this morning on the coast of Maine I felt like I use to feel when I walked the barnyard of my boyhood farm.

For most of my 46 years (65 now), good health has been an integral part of my life, my lifestyle, and my living. I grew up on a homestead where we eat homemade, home grown everything; drank clear, clean spring water from our own wells, and breathed healthy, homestead air. While others have battled various diseases and ailments most of their lives, I have suffered from few afflictions. I contribute that health to the habits of the homestead and a gracious God. I have spent more days visiting people in the hospital than I have spent in the hospital myself. Other than a few minor setbacks, like the removal of my tonsils when I was a tot, the surgeon's scalpel has not touched my body. I haven't had to live on medication, and I go to sleep naturally, why? I feel it is because of the good start I got in life from a homestead health.

Health is as much habit, as it is habitat. I lived in a place where nourishing food was a part of very meal, breakfast, dinner, and supper. Sometimes I liked it sometimes I didn't, but there were no alternatives! I didn't think about it then, but I ponder on it now. Could that be the reason we seem to have such a health crisis in our land today? Most of our meals today come from California or Florida or some far off and distant country; thousands of miles away. In a yesteryear long since passed, I ate home grown vegetables, ate home grown meats, and snacked on homemade sweets. I lived in a house where we went to bed early, and got a good night's sleep before we rose to hard days working and laboring doing exercising chores and healthy labors. My strength and vitality was not wasted on late night parties. My stamina and vigor was not lost on late night television either. I awoke to the rising sun and a rooster's crow, refreshed and invigorated by a deep, peaceful, restful sleep. We even took naps in those days! I was not awakened by sirens and screams. I also worked and played (Yes, we believed that all work and no play did make Barry a dull boy!) in an environment that exercised the whole body. Body, soul, and spirit were strengthened on a daily bases by not only what we did, but more often by what we didn't do. Our entire being was shaped and molded by whom we worked with, but more often than not by those we didn't associate or hang around. We speak of air and water pollution affecting our health, but we also need to speak of mind pollution! What good is there to have a healthy body if you have a sick, immoral, wicked mind? John wrote in one of his tiny epistles this profound desire: *"I wish above all things that thou mayest prosper and be in health . . . "* (III John 2) Physical health combined with spiritual health happens when you eat the right things, and live around the right people. Amen!

40

Four Seasons

LOOKING BACK OVER THE years, I have often reflected on the blessing of being raised in a barnyard instead of on a boulevard. I am thankful for being reared in the country instead of the city. I am a proud American, a proud Maineaic, and an even prouder 'county' boy! Vance Havner once said, *"God made the country and man-made the town, and you certainly can see the difference!"*

I am grateful for memories of potato fields and cow pastures, for maple trees in the front yard and spruce trees in the backyard, for swallows in the barn and chickens in a coup. I can still see the American Crow soaring in the evening sky being chased by barn sparrows because they came to close to their nests. I can still hear the crickets in the field across the road and the bull frogs in the pond down the road. What a privilege I had to taste the homestead life before progress made the farm modernize and with that modernization made the farm stop being a dairy and potato farm.

I am thankful that I was trained to be a 'man' for all seasons. I type today on the threshold of another change of seasons in my home state of Maine. Within weeks, summer will come. Though I have my favorite, each of the four seasons were special in their own way in my northern Maine of the 1950s and 1960s. I loved the white world of winter, the sweet sounds of spring, the sunny scenes of summer, and the full, fall foliage of autumn. Winter was the silent season that kept me in, and made me thank the Good Lord that He didn't create one season. Spring was the season of rebirth and resurrection that remained me that no matter how tough and rough life could get that there is always a spring ahead for each of us. Summer was like the song says: "The good old summertime!" For it was in the summers of my youth when I recharged my body and refreshed my soul with the warmest of a summer sun; it never got too hot in the summer that we didn't enjoy the few days of great weather we got. Autumn was the season that could have a bit of all the other seasons in it; from falling leaves to falling snow (this was northern Maine remember), from spring-like temperatures to summer-like temperatures? For me the best of the best was what we would call "Indian Summer"! A new season is upon me again, but the memories of past seasons still fill my mind with fond thoughts.

As I reflect on these blessed seasons, I realize I owe much to the time that I was born (the middle of the 20th century). In my youth, I complained of God's timing thinking of other times in history that I could have been born over the age of my existence. However, as I have passed well into the half-century mark, I am thankful I was honored and had the privilege to have been born when I was and where I was: a family homestead. So if I have any advice for those who might be traveling the road behind me, it would be this. Take the time to enjoy every day, every season. The days and seasons wax and wane so quickly that unless you stop to watch the seasons change you will miss most of the joys of life. The seasons pass with their own special songs and savors, and unless you take the time to learn their melodies and experiences their taste you might miss the very best that life has to offer. Summer is upon me again, but I will blink twice and tomorrow will arrive and it will be autumn. One breath after that and it will be wintertime again, and winter will huff and puff for a few moments and will blow spring back into my life, and before I know it summer has arrived again. Aren't you grateful God promised: "While the earth remaineth, seedtime and harvest, and cold and heat, summer and winter, and day and night shall not cease." (Genesis 8:22) Four seasons for a man for all seasons!

41

Noontime Nap

THE TITLE OF MY Sunday message was 'Napping at Noon'. I had been inspired by these words from Mrs. Charles Cowman: "We have lost the art of 'resting at noon'. Many are slowly succumbing to the strain of life because they have forgotten how to rest. The steady stream, the continuous uniformity of life, is what kills. Rest is not a sedative for the sick, but a tonic for the strong. It spells emancipation, illumination, transformation. It saves us from becoming slaves even to good works!" I had my title, the theme, and the text: *"Where thou makest thy flock to rest at noon."* (Song of Solomon 1:7) But what would be my opening illustration to my flock at the Emmanuel Baptist Church? Webster defines 'nap' as "to doze or sleep lightly for a short time". How my Dad could nap, and what a better introduction for a homestead homily than my father's napping!

Wendell E. Blackstone was a tireless worker on the family farm in Perham, Maine. For decades (over five of them), he rose before dawn to milk the Holstein herd. He did more work before breakfast than most men do all day. In the fall during potato harvest, he would rise even earlier to get the chores done, so that he could have the first row of spuds dug before the sun came up. Likewise, the end of the day was as busy as the beginning of the day for my Dad, as he once again milked the cows and finished up his daily chores. In the summer during haying season, the sun would set before Dad sat! Whether working in the field or forest, he always cut down all the wood that would be needed for the long

Maine winter, Dad was a hard worker, but where did he get the extra strength to go from dawn to dusk; 24-7 as they say today?

When I was a boy I thought it strange that Dad napped at noon. From as early as I can remember lunch was always at eleven o'clock. Unless it was harvest time or planting time, Dad always came home for lunch and without fail after a hearty meal he would go into the living room and lay down on the couch in the corner. He might read the newspaper or look at the mail for a minute or two, but within a short time he would be asleep. I have yet to meet another individual that could or can go to sleep faster than my father! His cat nap lasted between twenty to thirty minutes and before you could get to the door he was up and out and at work again. He never over-slept; he never had to be wakened, for it seemed my Dad had an internal alarm clock and when it was time to return to work it went off. That recharge, renewal at noon seemed to give him the boost to work on through a hard afternoon and if needed a long evening.

Dad didn't just nap at home. I remember seeing him stretched out on the Old John Deere tractor seat at noon after a long morning digging potatoes. I remember seeing him setting on a potato barrel leaning against a wall in the old potato house napping at noon after a morning putting up potatoes for shipping. I remember seeing him laid out under the big elm trees by the cow barn during haying season catching a few winks after mother had brought him lunch from home. When I was much younger than I am today, I thought my Dad must be weak having to take a nap at noon. I would play, read through my noon hour feeling I didn't need a rest. But know I see that it was that midday snooze that allowed my Dad to labor with such intensity all those many years, way up into his upper eighties. He was not weak, but wise! God created us with the need for rest. Not just one day in seven to rest, for I finally figured out because my Dad was a dairy farmer and one in seven was not possible for him; he compensated on a daily bases by taking a nap at noon which became his Sabbath rest!

42

Refreshing Rain

THE WEATHERMAN SAYS IT'S going to rain. I like when the rain falls; *'in every life a little rain must fall!'* I learned on the family farm just how important and precious the rain can really be, for the refreshing rain was always in season on the homestead, except, perhaps, during haying season! Its benefits were always greater than its liabilities, particularly if it was a gentle overnight rain. Driving downpours could be disastrous, but a soft summer shower was ideal and always welcomed. My memory stills recalls the sound of pitter/patter on our homestead home in the evening just after going to bed. The small raindrops would wash the windows in my bedroom, but more importantly they were soaking the soil with life giving moisture that would nourish the plants and soften the ground for whatever task we needed to perform the next morning. I would fall asleep with the satisfaction that our Good God was giving His creation a good drink: "*. . . who prepareth rain for the earth . . .* " (Psalm 147:8)

The next day after the rain clouds had passed by the grass seemed greener, the leaves on the trees seemed fuller, the crops seemed happier, and the flowers around the farm seemed more beautiful. If the rain came after a short drought, the potato plants in the side field would spring back to life overnight, the oats by the cow barn would head out, and the clover in the back pasture would smell sweeter. Everything that had been dusty before would have been washed clean and sparkling. The air smelt fresher and the land looked spotless. The dryness of the days past had been exchanged with a restoration and rejuvenation that could only be described as divine!

Everybody on the homestead felt the renewal equally, a renewal that only a rain can bring. I have watched the Holstein herd bath unaffected in the middle of the pasture under a spring shower. I have witnessed my dog Rover barking for joy in the midst of an August downpour after a long, hot summer with little rain. I have worked through a rain to get a field picked clean of rocks, ready for planting and now that the early rains had come the plants would root and sprout. Rain often cooled the atmosphere and the task you were doing when the heat of summer arrived; there is something quite marvellous about a timely rain, a needed shower, yes, evens a drenching downpour.

I learned on the homestead to like the sound of rain, to listening to the rain, to watch it rain, but I also learned to fish in the rain. There are a lot of activities you can't do in the rain, like hay and hoe and harvest, but I have found that some of the best times I have had fishing was in the rain. Fully exposed and fully extended down deep in a babbling brook; standing knee deep in a creek, what a wonderful feeling to raise your eyes to the sky and feel the touch of heaven's dew on your face. The tiny raindrops exploding in the stream have always made me excited because it often makes the brook trout in your favorite pool excited. Engulfed in the grandeur of the forest, catching a trout or salmon in the rain is a bonus I have experienced many times in my life, and I hope I will experience it many more times, just like the times on the homestead when we couldn't work in the rain, but we could go fishing in the rain!

A country cloudburst, a summer shower, a day-long drizzle, or a drenching downpour are just some of the ways a rural rain might affect your life. Each contained the one ingredient that makes the county, the country: water. Precipitation or condensation, call it what you will. Rainstorm or thunderstorm, call it as you see it. From sprinkles to showers, from drizzling to dripping, God's rain is the only cure I know for a drought!

43

Summer Storm

As summer moves slowly towards August, the heat and humidity have intensified here in the coastal city of Ellsworth. All the surrounding lawns, colored in a grassy green by spring showers in May and June, are gone. The searing sun of July has turned the area brown as nature dies of thirst. Shade less soil cries out for rain. The 'dog-days' of summer have arrived here, as they did on the family farm in Perham in the summers of my youth when *"He . . . raiseth the stormy wind."* (Psalm 107:25)

Sometimes, the first sign that a storm was on the way was a silent stillness. Suddenly the dry, hot air would stop blowing through the ever-green trees already hanging limp from lack of moisture. The song birds had even stopped singing as they tried to conserve their energy and seek a shady stoop against the steadily rising midsummer temperatures. Even the normal farm work was suspended; just too hot to work out-of-doors, but there was always something to do in-doors! All eyes were lifted skyward in hopes that the clouds building off the western horizon were filled with water?

As the bellowing black clouds moved into the area and blocked out the menacing rays of the sun, a bright, colorful streak of light exploded over the homestead. Thunder followed; rumbling down through the hollows to the north and tumbling over the hills to the east. Again and again the lighting crashed over the farm as the fields and forests to the west were aglow with a celestial glow. With each ignition, thunder shook the ground where I was standing in the wide doors of the cow barn. With the coming of the clouds, the wind once again began to blow heavily, announcing the approaching summer storm. How often I had watched a storm's creation from my favorite spot to witness one of God's greatest acts of nature. The protection of the barn would keep me dry, but the massive doors would also allow me to see the storm in all its grandeur and glory. Each time I stood in that doorway I stood amazed at the spectacular elements of a summer storm: made of stillness, of sound, and sheets of fire, and all that even before the water.

As far as my eye could see, the storm clouds had taken over the sky and the sod below it. What was so fascinating was that just a few hours before the sky were a July blue without a cloud to be seen. Now the darkness, comparable to a moon-lit night, was only illuminated by the electrical energy sweeping the landscape periodically at the sky edge of the storm. Despite the awesome show of power, the homestead was still dusty and drab after a prolonged period of drought. Minute by minute passed as the thunder and lighting and wind dominated the barnyard, the backyard, and the front yard of the farm. But amidst the numbing noise, another sound began to vibrate through the top of the barn. At first, it was only a gentle tapping sound, but in time it built to a heavy pounding sound. Is there anything more pleasant than rain on a roof, it is a stirring, satisfying sound that penetrates through one's body into one's soul! (Footnote: The last such storm I witnessed was in India in 2012. I had arrived in the monsoon season and for a 12 day stretch I watched one of these storms every afternoon. Indians hate such storms, but I basked in the glory of such a sound, a sight, and a shower for nearly two weeks!)

Raindrops began to fall at my feet as I stepped back deeper into the barn. I could hear the tiny water droplets hitting the windowpanes, as the heavens open up and the rain clouds dumped their contents, drenching the thirsty topsoil. Cloudburst after cloudburst pour on Perham the life giving moisture that would fill the soil, until the ground couldn't take any more; the drink has turned into *'my cup runneth over!'* And as fast as it blew in, it blew out. As quick as it came, it was quickly gone. The clouds soon disappeared and the sun reemerged as hot and humid as before, but a new world greeted me as I exited the front of the barn. The summer storm had worked a miracle; even the birds were singing!

44

Salutatorian Sylvia

IT HAS BECOME A sad day in Maine education when the top high school hero is the basketball star, the football champion, the baseball all-star instead of the valedictorian! What is more tragic is that most valedictorians, if they had a choice, would choose to be an athletic star verses an academic scholar. I must admit when I was a boy I too got caught up in the athletic mania that has been sweeping across our land for a very long time now. As I strove to be the best at baseball and basketball, soccer and cross country, I had a sister who looked beyond the temporary and excelled in academics, and concluded her high school career as the first salutatorian of the homestead.

We live in a land where brawn is idolized more than brains. We live in a country where we pay a football coach more than we pay an English teacher. *(My sister Sylvia was a high school English teacher for over forty years!)* The center of education is now the football gridiron or the basketball court or the baseball field instead of the classroom! Is it any wonder that the youth of today are so unprepared for the real world when our society has so distorted what is important and what is simply a game? Is it any wonder that our young people get distracted when the television makes *"the athletic field heaven and the star athlete god?"* When perfecting a jump shot or a fast ball or a goal line stand is more important than perfecting your writing skills or your math skills? When practicing a corner kick or a batting swing or a throwing pass is more important than practicing the piano or your times tables? When the athlete is so exalted above the academic that the

Homestead Homilies

backcourt artist can draw more spectators than the musical artist, something is wrong, seriously wrong with such our society. I like what was said by a concerned father when he concluded: *"that he had spent forty thousand dollars on his son's education and he only got a 'quarter-back!'"*

I didn't know it then, but I know it now; that during my boyhood it was my sister who was the real star of our family. Oh, I went five for five in a high school baseball game including a home run, but my sister getting all "A's" on her report card was better; where mine was an afternoon delight! Sure I scored 34 points in an overtime basketball win, but my sister's academic achievements were far reaching and far lasting; where mine was a one night thrill! Sure I scored a goal in only my second high school soccer game, but my sister scored higher, much higher on her SITs; where mine was just a momentary joy. Sure it takes discipline to run cross-country, but I learned very early in college that it takes more discipline to study Greek or write a paper. I see now that it was my sister Sylvia who was the real disciplined person in our childhood; I did that which came the easiest to me. To achieve academic superiority in a class or a school was then as it is now overlooked by most. Wouldn't it be great instead of the local six o'clock sports scores, the academic scores on that day's tests would be given out across the airwaves? That we would start honoring the academic sisters of the world instead of the athletic brothers would be nice! Even the Apostle Paul highlighted and underlined this concept years ago, centuries before football and basketball: "*. . . for bodily exercise profiteth little . . .* " (I Timothy 4:8). I know now the real scholar, heroine of my childhood lived in my house, sat across the table from me every morning, and help me patiently with my homework and academic struggles. Sylvia might have only received the salutatorian award when she graduated from Washburn District High School in 1968, but as for me, I see now she was my valedictorian, and as you can see from this homestead homily, she still is!

45

Pump Priming

I AM CAUGHT IN my study at the Emmanuel Baptist Church in Ellsworth, Maine as the snow of a snowy winter piles up outside my windows. It has been snowing for 26 straight hours, and it has turned our coastal town into a winter wonderland of snow piles, snow banks, and snow-covered streets. Do you remember the snow scene from *"It's a Wonderful Life?"* For a snow lover like we, it is a beautiful sight and site! I like snow, but I love spring. So I have decided that while it finishes snowing and blowing, didn't I tell you the wind is up making this an official blizzard, I will take another mental trip back to the northeastern corner of Maine where I use to live as a lad in my boyhood. This time my homestead homily is about a Perham pump that I had to prime in order to get some of the sweetest tasting and most pristine liquid to drink.

The old cast iron pump was painted red as I recall, and its long handle took all the strength you had as a boy to move it up and down. I remember it was easier when you had help from a cousin or two, but a sister would do! It pulled water from a deep well of water under the homestead, but towards the end of its existence it had to be primed before you could get any water out of it at all. It wasn't that the well was dry, but the pump was dry and worn and old, so you had to pour a little water from another source down it to get the water flowing again. Even then, I recall having to do a whole lot of pumping to get a drink of water, but the water was worth the work. Over the years I have thought of that old pump many times, but not like David desiring a drink of water from a homestead well (II Samuel 23:13-17). My thoughts have been more around the idea that how often in my life I have been like that old pump, in need of priming!

As a pump is attached to a refreshing source of water like an underground spring, so too is the human life attached to good things. Granados thoughts, good deeds, grand dreams, and great achievements are buried deep in the human soul, put there by God's breath (Genesis 2:7). They are there like the water is there, but how to get them to the surface is the great question? Often I have worked and struggled to get some refreshment, either for myself or others, only to come up dry, to feel dry. The fault is not with life, as with the water, but with the pump, me! I am a dry pump that needs priming. My priming more often than not comes from others. I remember pumping on that old iron handle as my sister poured water down through the top of the pump. How often I have been unproductive, uninspired when my wife, or a friend has said something encouraging to help me push on, press on and has made my spirit flow again. How often when I couldn't think of anything to write about or a sermon topic to prepare that I pushed back from my computer or my desk and picked up a book by Vance Havner and my lethargic brain was primed again by something I read. Most of my memories have been primed from some source borrowed from another pump, as with this homily!

The fire I spread in my sermons are often kindled from someone else's fireplace. This is why I like to read good books, listen to good music, look at good pictures, and breathe good-old country air. They are the priming of my pump. But we should never forget that priming is not enough. My sister could pour gallon after gallon into that old pump and never get a drop of water in return unless I pumped and pumped and pumped. It takes priming and pumping to make an old-fashion well work. It takes team work to extract water from the bottom of a deep well. And it takes similar team work to get through life. Solomon wrote of this 'pump priming precept' in Ecclesiastes 4:9–12. Check it out!

46

"Great" Grandmother

AREN'T YOU GETTING SICK and tired of all these 'success' magazines and television specials that are now being published and broadcast about the world's best? You know the ones, they have feature articles and interviews with titles like, "How I made a Million Dollars before I was Thirty", "I Am a Teenager Super Star", or "Fame and Fortune My Way!" I would like to share with you in this homily an individual who played the game of life brilliantly, but missed all the headlines and newscasts!

I am rather tired of the stereotype success story that tells of the traditional 'rags to riches' tale; how their brilliance in a sport or finances either made them a fortune or famous. I would tell you of a lady who was good, but not because it paid. Glenna Esty Blackstone is one of those splendid souls who was planted in a small corner of the world to be an example to me and others. Her story will never make the periodicals because her type of story isn't sensational enough. Her tale doesn't contain enough hair-raising adventures or secret sins or terrible habits overcome to get published or proclaimed except by an admiring grandson. Gram's greatest fault in the area of news was she was faithfully good and we know good news never makes the nightly news any longer because sin sells, evil is entertaining and wicked women sell papers and air-time!

Grandma had no Pollyanna kind-of-life. She lived most of her life in small towns in Northern Maine doing low-level jobs: school teacher and farmer's wife. She raised two boys and cared for her mother, in her mother's home, until she died in her 90s.

She out lived her husband by 28 years, but widowhood never took away her sense of humor or her will to live. She had done enough work in her life to be in a wheelchair or a nursing home yet she lived into her 100th year still living in the house my grandfather built for her in the 1920s. Through bad potato years and bad milk prices she stayed good, honest and trustworthy, not because it paid, but because it was the right thing to do.

Glenna was the 'salt of the earth' (Matthew 5:13) and a 'light in the world' (Matthew 5:14) and her character was the moral and spiritual cement that held our family together for decades after Granddad Carroll died so suddenly in 1975. Her faithfulness and consistency spanned over five decades of my life, so I am without excuse to say, *"It is impossible to go from obscurity to prosperity and not lose your integrity!"* Grandfather left her one of the richest woman in Perham, but you would never have known it by her life, living, and lifestyle. I am no making her out to be a saint because she experienced her share of doubt, fear and perplexing turns in her life that made her sad and sorrowful, but she still pressed on, pushed forward and stayed good in heart and action and in my opinion, actually better, yes, the best!

Vance Havner once said, *"It is a precious thing whenever you find it, this goodness that goes unpaid. These are the heroes without the halos, the souls that sing while they stifle sobs and look upward through tearful eyes. Often wondering why things go as they do, they do not give up the dream because they cannot make it come true. These are the real successes. They are good in spite of what they got- good because the pursuit of goodness is sweeter than the possession of everything else!"* That was my "great' grandmother! A lady who was there at every turn of my road for over 50 years encouraging me to be good, no matter the cost, no matter the reward, because being good and gracious and generous is reward in itself. She never made the papers, she never made the news, but her fame and fortune was laid up in heaven. (Matthew 6:19–21)

47

Devote Dad

WENDELL ESTY BLACKSTONE RULED his home with a loving influence, a tempered authority, and a godly grace. He is a true sire in every since of the word: a man of integrity. He is a closed hearted man who taught his children discipline, faithfulness, and respect through his easy going life, living, and lifestyle; though not a stern disciplinarian; a stern look or a single word of rebuke was sufficient to correct the wayward child. Though he lived in the days when it was not fashionable to show physical affection to one's child, his love came through in many other ways. I can see him patiently listening in silence as mother would describe an escapade I had done that particular day and though he might follow it up with a warning, it was always delivered with a smile.

In my boyhood farming and faith dominated the homestead. Dad was a devote Baptist who centered his extra moments around his local church. He practiced and preached a strict adherence to the Bible order of things. Sunday was for milking and messages from the Word of God. We said 'grace' before every meal and foul language was never tolerated. (I struggle to remember a single time a curse word was ever used on the homestead.) Don't get me wrong, for Dad was never one of these always sober individuals, always serious Calvinists. Dad loved to laugh and I can still see him doubled over in laughter as he watched the 'Red' Skeleton show on television. He loved a good, clean joke anytime, workplace or worship place. Dad had great spiritual fortitude and plenty of human dignity to go along with his great sense of humor.

His voice, when you heard it because he was a man of few words, was wonderfully gentle and deep. When the issue got serious, his speech was slow and impassioned with thought and wisdom. I only saw him angry on the rarest of occasions. When convinced in a cause or a truth, Wendell would stand against the devil himself and a legion of his demons, if he thought himself right. He taught me that convictions were worth everything, and a man without convictions was not worth much!

Wendell Esty Blackstone is a man totally indifferent to possessions, or things of any kind. He never got trapped into the 'more is better' philosophy that has haunted and harassed his nation for most of his life. He still lives the simplest of lifestyles: *"Therefore take no thought, saying, What shall we eat? Or, What shall we drink? Or, Wherewithal shall we be clothed?"* (Matthew 6:31) He is the typical home-body who has travelled just a few times from his homestead. He like Paul learned early to be content in whatever (Philippians 4:11–12) he had or wherever he was.

Despite his farmer image, Dad has held every office in the ministry of the church except pastor. He was given the office of deacon early on in his married life and the words of Paul ring true of him: *"For they that have used the office of deacon will purchase to themselves a good degree."* (I Timothy 3:13) Public or private, Dad has maintained his patient character, his quiet demeanor, and his caring nature before family and friends. The self-appointed 'welcoming committee' chairman of Perham, he takes it upon himself to visit and help every new resident of his hometown. It is perhaps in this unseen area of his life that he has proven himself to be the most devote. Devote to church and Christ, devote to children and wife, devote to family and friends, but most devote to the stranger and pilgrim that crosses his path. Dad follows religiously this statute from the Levitical book of Moses: *". . . that a man shall devote unto the Lord of all that he hath . . . every devoted thing is most holy unto the Lord."* (Leviticus 27:28) (Footnote: my Dad has maintained this discipline into his 93rd year. His residence is now a Veteran's home in Caribou, Maine. Despite the onset of dementia, Dad has kept his core character!)

48

Frosty Frost

ONLY THOSE WHO LIVE in the northern hemisphere know of the strength and sparkle of frost. I remember walking on my father's farm in northern Maine in early October to find a white film (we often called it a 'killing frost') over my world, but I also recall the same thing happening in September! No, snow had not fallen, but the fabled frost of fall had. The temperatures had dropped dramatically over night so everything was covered in frost. The landscape around the barnyard was transformed into a crystal castle of breathless beauty: "... *by the breath of God frost is given."* (Job 37:10)

What made a frosty morning in Perham so beautiful was the sun. When the rays of the sun hit the frost covered twigs of the birch tree, or the needles of the fur tree, the frost surrounding the homestead exploded into a whitish glitter. As the twinkling lights in the heavenly sky on a dark night, the fields and forest covered in white acted like a massive prism refracting the sun's rays. All the colors of the prism could be seen in nature's morning light show, and it is still unmatched by the technology of man, despite his lights and lasers! What a sight and site unfolded before that barnyard boy's eyes; a recollection, as you can see, that is still amazing and astonishing to him to this day.

Frost like dew is created on clear, cold, calm nights. When the sun goes down and the atmosphere cools and the night air cannot hold as much moisture as the daylight air; when the night air becomes saturated and the dew point is reached, frost forms. In actuality, frost is formed when water vapor touches a cold surface.

If the land mass is above freezing then dew is formed, but if below, as it often happens between October and April in northern Maine, then frosty frost will be the result.

Frost, however, has a short life even in Maine, especially in the strength of an early autumn sunrise. The sun's rays are still too powerful for the fallish frost, so the frost hides. It finds protection in the heart of the earth. As the days grow shorter and the nights grow longer, the frost has a longer life, for it buries itself deeper into the ground. When the snow holds off, for snow will act as a blanket to the ground and will resist the penetration of the frost, but unrestricted, frost can play havoc, and despite its beauty, it can be a bother and bring about countless difficulties in autumn and later in spring!

I remember having to reset fence posts in the spring around the pastures of Perham because the frost had lifted them from their holes. It was one of the reasons Grandpa and Dad often had us take up the fence line in the fall, for they knew that a good Maine frost would force us to redo the line in the spring anyway. Who of us hasn't seen a porch door or a panty door become distorted because frost has changed the foundation under it just a bit? The parsonage of the Emmanuel Baptist Church has a back porch door that remains unlocked throughout the winter because of that kind of effect! We are only troubled by this as long as frost is around, but once gone, the door returns to normal and we know spring has arrived. And who of us has not traveled the bumpy roads of a typical spring in Maine when the frost begins to come out of the ground under the roadway. Frost and potholes go hand in hand in Maine. My driveway and the lanes around the church are showing signs of frost heaves and all we are experiencing is a January thaw; the real battle in mud season is the escape of frost from its wintry abode. How does something so fragile in the fall become so strong in the spring? Such is the mystery of nature when beauty turns into brute force. The world needs to understand this concept because the sparkling Jesus of Galilee will become the powerful, killing King next time around!

49

Clover Concepts

BEING RAISED ON A potato and dairy farm in the 1950s and 1960s, I had the privilege to work many days in the clover fields scattered around our 720 acre homestead. For decades, the farm had been run on a rotation-crop system. A field after two years of producing Katahdin potatoes was sown in oats and clover. The first year the oats would dominate, but the next year would bring in a field of the sweetest smelling cover crop there is! We had certain fields that only yielded hay because they were not suited for potatoes or oats, but the best cuttings of the summer for winter food for the Holstein herd where the fields sown in clover. To walk through a field of clover must be equal to a stroll through heaven with a divine aroma unmatched. It was also in those fields of clover that I learned many a valuable lessons from my earthly father that has assisted me well in the fieldwork I have been laboring in the pastorate. For it was in the clover fields of my youth that I learned about cutting a straight swath, taking time for proper preparation, and the importance of preventative maintenance.

Whether cutting, conditioning, or raking, Dad loved a full swath. Because of the crookedness of our field's contours, it was sometimes difficult to keep the swaths straight. Yet as one gained experience with the hay cutter, hay conditioner, or hay rake, one learned that by directing the tractor with the direction of the swath, the crooks and obstructions could be straightened out. So it is as we direct our lives through this world, we too can smooth out the crooks and turns by keeping a straight course and keeping our ultimate goals in the forefront: *". . . Make thy way straight before my face."* (Psalm 5:8)

Rare was the day that we could cut, condition, rake, and bale in the same day. A field of hay, especially clover, takes time to dry. If clover is put into storage to soon it will mold. It takes the sun and plenty of it; it takes the wind and plenty of it, to properly dry a field of clover. Despite the risk of showers and rain, it takes patience and preparation to wait the best time to bale. Father taught me the importance of patience with a field of clover, and so it is with life itself. How many rewards have we lost because of impatience, a premature harvest? Wise is the man that is patient enough to wait for life's rewards to mature and dry: *"Ye have heard of the patience of Job."* (James 5:11)

Because I was born in the mechanical age, haying was done with mostly machines; granted, in my day we still didn't have the means to pick up the bales of hay with machines, but that would come. About the only hand labor was picking up the bales of clover and putting them on a truck for transport to the cow barn, the rest was done with tractors and baling equipment. Each piece of machinery was only as good as the maintenance provided. I still recall the lessons Dad gave me in the proper greasing of the rake, the proper care for the conditioner, and the necessary sharpening of the cutter. Before we took these baling machines into the field we always checked them over in the old machine shop tucked in a wooded area north of the homestead. Preventive maintenance is important for all farm equipment, and it is equally important for our body, soul, and spirit (I Thessalonians 5:23). Maintaining the members of my God-given body will allow me to make a full swath in life. The danger in going into the field of the world without a properly maintained body will result in a break down. Paul wrote of this: *"But I keep under my body, and bring it into subjection: lest that by any means, when I have preached to others, I myself should be a castaway!"* (I Corinthians 9:27) Baling equipment or Barry's equipment properly maintained is of vital importance to both.

50

Hill Homily

JUST RECENTLY I SANG that classic Church hymn: "The Church in the Wildwood", at a nursing home service I was conducting in Ellsworth. Besides being one of my father-in-law's favorite songs, it is also the anthem of every country loving church member. I was fortunate to have been raised on a farm in rural Maine were *"the little white church in the vale"* could be seen from the top of a hill on the homestead. That hymn and that hill came together to make this homily. *"There's a church in the valley by the wildwood, no lovelier spot in the dale, no place is so dear to my childhood, as the little white church in the vale."* Don't get me wrong, I know the original hymn used the color 'brown', but for me my valley church was white!

In my boyhood, I remember fondly the times I use to climb the hill near my grandparent's home (a house I own now) and gaze down into the hamlet of Perham. Despite the few houses nestled in that green valley, the dominate focal point was the steeple of the First Baptist Church building. Like the hymn, it too was surrounded by trees (wildwoods). Its tall white spire stood alone high above the skyline of my home town. Each time I return (as I have been doing for 47 years now) to that hill and witness again that tranquil scene, I wonder why I ever left that fair haven for the turmoil of the town and the confusion of the city? *"How sweet on a clear Sabbath morning, to list to the clear ringing bell, its tones so sweetly are calling!"*

I live today just a block from a church building that still rings its bells on Sunday morning. They sound heavenly against the noise of the coastal city I have lived in for a quarter of a century now. Despite the divine sound, those city bells have never drawn me to their sanctuary, but they simply take me back to the days when a single bell from a Baptist belfry use to echo down through the Salmon Brook Valley and call me and my family to worship. Those were the days when people really practiced there faith and the meeting house was just a building; the church were the people, the brotherhood of Christ (I Peter 2:17). Those were the days when the body of Christ rarely forsook the assembly of themselves together (Hebrew 10:25). *"Oh, come to the church in the wildwood, to the trees where the wild flowers bloom, where the parting hymn will be chanted, we will weep by the side of the tomb."*

This remembrance is not mere sentiment or nostalgia for "the good-old days". It is a hope and a prayer that those who still have a chance to worship in that "little white church in the vale" will realize it is they that have changed, not the view from the hill. I like what Vance Havner once observed: *"It has not dawned upon most of us that we do not need some new thing so much as some old thing that would be new if anybody would just try it. We had better get out of the novelty shop and return to the antique shop!"* And old hymn sung from an old hill overlooking an old house of God might be exactly what is needed to solve an old hostility or an old grudge. *"Oh, come, come, come, come, come to the church in the wildwood, Oh, come to the church in the vale, no spot is so dear to my childhood, as the little white church in the vale."*

Periodically over the years I have returned from my travels to revisit that 'little white church in the vale' in my hometown of Perham, Maine. Lately however, I have enjoyed more the view from the hill than the view from the pew. Too many friends and family I once worshipped with are gone. My father-in-law is gone as I have wept by the side of his tomb. Each passing year, 'The Church in the Wildwood' has become a parting hymn!

Conclusion
Soil Sermons

My forefathers picked a tough terrain to establish a homestead in the year of 1861. Rugged, rocky ridges cover the landscape I call home, my homestead. On those stony hilltops grew stand upon stand of fur and spruce and maple and elm and pine. Once the land was cleared, the soil had to be reconditioned to raise potatoes instead of poplar and oats instead of oak for now the priority of the land was Holsteins and homesteaders. The granite knolls had to be recovered with rich soil so the family and its animals wouldn't starve. So as my ancestors looked at their stony, sun-baked ridges and wondered if they could ever make the land productive, they got to work!

Remember, this transformation didn't take place a few years ago, but over 150 years ago. Modern man and his mighty machines hadn't been invented yet. Modern man and his 'much' money wasn't a reality yet. All my forefathers had was human ingenuity, a strong back, and a few oxen. Tons and tons of topsoil couldn't be hauled in from the more fertile plains along the Aroostook River, so the tilling and the tending began. Lacking then was all the fuss and fumes and fanfare of the modern farmer. Left to the founders of Perham was their strong-will and the dung from their cattle. Roots and rocks were replaced inch by inch. As the ground was exposed to the sun and the showers, the soil began to build itself up with nutrients. As the seasons passed each year the land was carefully and lovingly sowed and spread with manure. As it was plowed and harrowed and disked again and again, the soil began to change. Grass and clover now needed to feed the increasing herd was plowed under and during the winter slumber, the soil enriched itself as it prepared itself for another spring planting.

The thick blanket of manure each year gave back to the land the minerals lost, taken from the soil by the previous crop. The turned over mulch combined with the sun's heat and the rain's moisture created the organic materials that would allow another year's crop. Instead of a thin, topsoil that quickly ran off in a sudden downpour, the ground was now able to hold the rain and store the moisture. Each passing year that protective covering resulted in the soil growing richer and darker until the time I came along (1951)! The fields were producing larger and larger crops of potatoes and abundant harvests of oats and clover; besides feeding a Holstein herd that numbered well over a hundred head on some of the richest pastureland in the county!

I recall days of my youth when I would be found; one with the soil. Hand-hoeing potato rows made you one with the soil. A final picking of rocks on an oat field made you one with the soil. Picking potatoes in the fall made you one with the soil. I don't know how many hundreds of pounds of Blackstone soil went through my fingers as a lad, but this I know: it even tasted good! A carrot or a radish or a potato with a bit of Blackstone homestead dirt on it was a favorite seasoning for me in my childhood. And now after 50 years of preaching, I realize that the soil and the sod of the homestead produced more than memories and reminiscences, but a whole collection of homestead homilies, soil sermons, meadow meditations, land lessons that have been the instruction book of my life. It is my prayer that these 'homilies' might bring you back to a simpler time when a homily was heard during the week as well as on Sunday. When a sermon was shared by an encounter with somebody other than your pastor!

Barry Blackstone

www.ingramcontent.com/pod-product-compliance
Lightning Source LLC
Chambersburg PA
CBHW070505090426
42735CB00012B/2676